HAROLD ADAMS INNIS

Portrait of a Scholar

HAROLD ADAMS INNIS

HAROLD ADAMS INNIS

Portrait of a Scholar

Donald Creighton

UNIVERSITY OF TORONTO PRESS
TORONTO BUFFALO LONDON

© University of Toronto Press 1978
Toronto Buffalo London
Reprinted in paperback 2015
ISBN 978-0-8020-6329-8 (paper)
LC 58-854

PREFACE

THIS SMALL BOOK is my contribution to the understanding of a great Canadian scholar. It has been a deep satisfaction for me to write it; but it could not have been written without the encouragement and co-operation of the members of the Innis family, and of Innis's colleagues and friends. I should like in particular to thank Mary Quayle Innis, who gave me access to her husband's private correspondence and the short memoir of his boyhood and early manhood which he dictated in the last months of his life. Vincent Bladen, who succeeded him as chairman of the Department of Political Economy at the University of Toronto, and Jane Ward, who for a number of years was his secretary, have been most helpful in collecting useful material for this study from the departmental files; and Innis's correspondents in Canada, the United Kingdom, and the United States have responded generously to a request for his letters. I am grateful for all this kind assistance, and also for the fruitful discussions of Innis's life and work which I have had with his colleagues, Vincent Bladen, Alexander Brady, and S. D. Clark, with a colleague of earlier days, Gilbert E. Jackson, and with a former student, J. G. Crean.

D. G. CREIGHTON

University of Toronto
August, 1957

PREFACE TO THE PAPERBACK EDITION

HAROLD ADAMS INNIS died early in the morning of November 8, 1952. The University of Toronto was well aware of the fact that it had lost one of its greatest scholars and teachers, and it took appropriate steps to mourn his death and honour his memory. The funeral service, which was attended by a very large congregation of staff and students from all faculties and colleges in the University, took place on the tenth. Then and later there were tributes to the importance of Innis's work and influence; but it was felt from the beginning that these verbal honours ought to be followed by some more durable memorial. In the next few days, Innis's friends and colleagues were busy discussing two principal methods of commemoration: first, the organization of his papers and manuscripts and the republication of some of his books; and second, the establishment of Innis scholarships and fellowships, or the founding of a Harold Innis chair in Political Economy, or an Innis Research Centre. As yet, nobody was sufficiently daring to suggest building an Innis College in his honour.

The first of these projects got under way a little earlier than the second. On November 10, Mary Innis, Harold Innis's wife, appointed a small committee, consisting of Delbert Clark, Tom Easterbrook, and myself, to advise her about the disposition of her husband's papers, manuscripts, and books. At first, Mary evidently expected that this small committee might itself discuss the various projects of commemoration with the University and the Rockefeller Foundation; but it speedily became clear that Messrs Easterbrook, Clark, and Creighton—none of whom was then head of a university department—simply did not possess enough authority or influence to carry out such negotiations on their own. The President of the University, Sidney Smith, may not even have been aware of our committee's existence. He must have felt, at any rate, that something more official and imposing was required. He decided to invite a number of senior members of the University to discuss the whole matter with him at a luncheon at the York Club on Friday, November 21.

It was a formidable gathering. The President, his assistant Claude Bissell, Principal Jeanneret of University College, A. R. Gordon, soon to be appointed Dean of the Graduate School, A. S. P. Woodhouse, Head of the Department of English at University College, and, of course, a large delegation from the Department of Political Economy, were all present. The various possible methods of commemoration—scholarships, fellowships, an Innis professorship, an Innis Research Centre—were all debated. President Smith showed himself interested and sympathetic, but carefully non-committal. Despite his genial and expansive manner, he was a very cautious financier. Prudence may not have been in his nature; but before coming to Toronto he had been President of the University of Manitoba, and prudence had certainly been drilled into him during his years at Winnipeg.

He was the first president to be appointed after a Royal Commission of Inquiry had revealed the appalling fact that the University of Manitoba's former Bursar and Chairman of the Board had embezzled nearly a million dollars of university money. A regime of rigid economy was introduced at once. There was no money at Manitoba for anything but the most basic academic necessities. For ten years, President Smith was forced to endure the inflexible, almost inquisitorial, system of cost accounting imposed by the financial authorities on the University's expenditure. He learnt economy and caution the hard way.

There may have been another reason for the President's prudent reserve. In all probability, he had not yet fully realized the extent of Harold Innis's influence with the great foundations in the United States; and in the 1950s the financial help of these foundations was vital to the success of any of the commemorative plans discussed at the luncheon at the York Club in November. A year earlier, the Massey Commission had recommended that a Canada Council should be established and supplied with adequate funds for the encouragement of the arts, letters, humanities, and social sciences in Canada. The Canada Council was the hope of the future for Canadian humanists and social scientists; but, in the autumn of 1952, its establishment was nearly five years ahead. Throughout nearly the whole of the 1950's, it was to the great American institutions—the Guggenheim Foundation, the Rockefeller Foundation, and the Carnegie Endowment for International Peace—that Canadian scholars had to turn for financial help.

The chief officers of these three great organizations probably knew Harold Innis better than any other academic figure in Canada. Henry A. Moe, the Secretary-General of the Guggenheim Foundation, asked his advice in awarding the Canadian fellowships. James T. Shotwell, the Director of the Division of Economics and History in the Carnegie Endowment, had made Innis his chief Canadian adviser in the planning of the great series of volumes on *The Relations of Canada and the United States*. The chief officers and consultants of the Rockefeller Foundation, notably Joseph Willits and Anne Bezanson, were equally well acquainted with him. Miss Bezanson came up to

Toronto for Harold's funeral, and two days later Delbert Clark and I went over to her hotel to discuss the problem of the Innis papers and the possibility of a research centre as a memorial to his achievement.

From the start it was obvious, at least to a small group of Harold's close associates and friends, that the Rockefeller Foundation was likely to look very favourably on any research project in Innis's honour. Once President Smith and his senior academic advisers had become aware of this fact, the University officially began to consider plans for a suitable memorial. In December, Vincent Bladen and Delbert Clark were still talking hopefully of a research centre. But the American foundations, like all other bodies with funds for deserving artists, writers, and scholars, were terrified at the thought of becoming entangled in a permanent commitment. Gradually, the University gave up all hope of an endowed Innis professorship or research centre; and late in April, 1953, when C. A. Ashley, then Acting Head of the Department of Political Economy, wrote to Willits in New York, he asked simply for a grant in aid of research in the social sciences at Toronto for a period of five years. On June 19, the Executive Committee of the Rockefeller Foundation authorized a grant of $215,000 for a programme of "research on the problems of Canadian development." The money was to be paid in annual instalments, exactly as Ashley had suggested, until 1958–59.

The lapse of a quarter century, including ten years of rapidly rising inflation, has made the Rockefeller grant look very small. But it was not small at the time; and the committee appointed to administer it, with Vincent Bladen as its chairman, made the money go a very long way indeed. A surprisingly large number of research appointments, summer fellowships, and grants in aid were made to senior and junior professors and to graduate students in economics, politics, history, and anthropology. The

Harold Innis Visiting Research Professorship, with what was then thought to be the very generous salary of $10,000 a year, was, of course, the most important appointment of all. It was awarded, first, to George E. Britnell, an economist at the University of Saskatchewan; next to A. G. Bailey, anthropologist and historian at the University of New Brunswick; and finally, to myself—though, as a member of the Department of History at the University of Toronto, I could hardly justify the title "Visiting Professor."

In the meantime, while all this tremendous activity in research was going on, the little committee, appointed by Mary Innis on November 10, 1952, had not been idle. It never found a way of dealing with the vast mass of manuscript on the press and communications generally, which Harold had left behind him; but there were other, more pressing, matters which it could and did attend to. Two of Innis's most important books—*The Cod Fisheries* and *The Fur Trade in Canada*—had long been out of print; and a large number of his essays, addresses, and introductions to works by other scholars had never been collected in book form. The committee, which soon came to include Donald Innis, Harold's son, and which enjoyed the expert help of Jane Ward, his former secretary, quickly busied itself with the problems of selection and editorial revision. Innis had been accustomed to annotate the margins of his published books with pertinent new facts, ideas, or references which had come to his attention after publication; and these comments were included in the revised edition of *The Cod Fisheries* which came out in 1954, the revised edition of *The Fur Trade in Canada* which followed two years later, and the revised edition of *Empire and Communications* which appeared in 1972. *Essays in Canadian Economic History*, a collection of no fewer than twenty-eight papers from a wide variety of sources, also appeared in 1956. Throughout this entire programme of publication, the main burden of selection and revision was borne by Mary Innis herself, with considerable assistance from Delbert Clark and Tom Easterbrook.

In all this endeavour I could do no more than act the part of a benevolent observer. My contribution, it was thought from the beginning, was to be something quite different: as early as the presidential luncheon at the York Club in November, 1952, Vincent Bladen and others had been urging me to do a "memoir" of Harold. I protested that I was an historian, not an economist or a political scientist, and that it would be impossible for me to do a satisfactory critical analysis of Innis's economic and political theories. These arguments seemed to carry conviction, and eventually it was decided that Alex Brady, Delbert Clark, and myself should all contribute to a single memorial volume, Brady dealing with politics, Clark with economics, and myself supplying a narrative account of the main events of Innis's life.

During the summer of 1956 I set to work on my share of this joint undertaking and finished it before the academic term began that autumn. My fellow authors and other critics said they liked my essay, but unfortunately it departed, in two important respects, from the plan which we had laid down for the memorial volume. It turned out to be considerably longer than had been intended, and it also discussed, though somewhat sketchily, the aspects of Innis's work which were supposed to be the special concern of my collaborators. Alex Brady and Delbert Clark who, if I remember rightly, had not yet begun their own essays, seized on these deviations from the original scheme and turned them into arguments for abandoning it altogether. My biographical sketch, they insisted, was itself sufficient to meet the need for a written memorial.

In the end these arguments convinced me. I did not relish the thought of making substantial cuts in my little biography, as I probably would have had to do in order to make room for two other contributions in a single volume. Also, having finished my own work, I was naturally eager to see it in print. I agreed to separate publication; but I thought then, and still think, that it was a pity the original design was given up. Much has been written about Innis since then, by people who knew him little or not at all. It seems unfortunate that Clark and Brady, two of his colleagues and close friends, did not record at any length their interpretations of his thought at a time when his memory was still very fresh in their minds.

This paperback reprint of *Harold Adams Innis: Portrait of a Scholar* is a photographic reproduction of the book as it was published in 1957. This means that I have been able to do no more than proofread the original text; but, even if changes had been possible, I doubt that I would have made them. In 1956 I wrote under a fresh, deep sense of personal bereavement and loss; and, after more than twenty years, these feelings are irrecoverable. I prefer to let the book stand as my original tribute to a good friend and a great scholar.

DONALD CREIGHTON

August 29, 1977

HAROLD ADAMS INNIS

Portrait of a Scholar

CHAPTER ONE

I

THE HOUSE stood a little below the crest of a long ridge. Ages before, the glacier had paused in its sluggish career southward; and the detritus of its moraine had solidified in the long low elevation which became known as Oak Ridge. To the north, the land fell away fairly sharply towards the line of the eighth concession of South Norwich; and to the south, beyond the crest of the hill, it spread out in a wide, gently rolling tableland which ended, less than a mile away and close to the narrow road of the ninth concession, in a deep wood of tall and whispering trees. The great pines of the original forest had been cut down long before, and the thick, interlaced roots of their stumps formed the farm's fences on either side; but chestnut, butternut, and hickory nut trees were still standing and the woodlot was thick with the dense vegetation of many maples. Here, and all over the rolling tableland, the earth—rich boulder clay and top-soil—was good; but northward, beyond the crest of the ridge, the seeping waters of the glacier had left a long drift of sand.

The slope down to the eighth concession road, about a fifth of a mile away, was disappointingly unproductive; but it had one gift which partly redeemed its niggardliness. It offered a tremendous view. From the steps of the small house perched near the crest of the ridge, one could see the wide landscape spread out in a simple, satisfying pattern of roads and fields, houses and barns, orchards and woodlots; and away to the north the blue border of the horizon was sombre with remoteness. Mary Adams Innis loved the view. It was the view which had impelled her to beg her newly married husband to build the house closer to the top of the hill. Often, in after years, when he urged his horses up the difficult slope through snow or mud, William Anson Innis regretted that he had built so far away from the concession road. But Mary had had her way. And the windows of the little house looked serenely out over the enormous landscape below it.

They had been married late in December, 1893, during the Christmas holiday season; and, for the winter months, William Innis brought his bride to his father's farm, which fronted on the tenth concession of South Norwich, almost directly south of the property which he was so soon to make his own. Already, for three generations, the Innises had been typical British North American pioneers. James Innis, the founder of the family, was a British soldier who had fought through the American Revolutionary War and who, like so many other veterans of the struggle, had been granted lands in the Province of New Brunswick. But the great farm on the banks of the Kennebecasis River was not to become the permanent home base of the Innises in North America; and some time fairly early in the nineteenth century—and family tradition has it about the year 1824—Isaac Innis, the veteran's son, made the incredible overland journey westward through New York State to the Province of Upper Canada. He settled in Blenheim Township, Oxford County, on what was almost certainly crown land. It was the second of the Innis struggles with the unbroken forest; but it was not to be the last. Some twenty years later, Samuel Innis, Isaac's son and the grandson of the British Army veteran, decided to move once more. This time the removal, from Blenheim Township to South Norwich Township in the same County of Oxford, was relatively short and unadventurous; but once again the farm was crown land, and once again, and for the third generation, Samuel accepted the terrible burdens of pioneer home-building. He married Sarah Stringham, a girl of Pennsylvania Dutch extraction, and in rapid succession they had a large family of twelve children, the eighth of whom, born in 1865, the year after the Quebec Conference, was called William Anson. William Anson represented the fourth generation of the North American Innises; he had behind him three-quarters of a century of effort and experience, and, late in 1893, when he married Mary Adams, he was still a youngish man, getting on for thirty years of age, slight, nearly six feet tall, with dark hair, a short dark beard and moustache, and a quiet, slow-spoken manner.

By the time the spring of 1894 broke in south-western Ontario, the newly married Innises had matured their plans. Mary was prominent in these discussions under the lamp-light in the long winter evenings; from the first she precipitated decisions and hastened action. She was a short, slight woman, a few years younger than her husband, with red hair, and the pale, fair complexion that often goes with it, and bright, intensely blue eyes. Her father, William Adams, had come to Canada from Roxboroughshire in Scotland: and Mary was the eldest of the four children of a marriage which he had contracted, late in life, with a young widow named Nancy Macdonald Easton. William Adams had had almost no formal training himself, but he strove to educate his children and to impress them with the enormous value of education; and when he died his daughter Mary used part of her small legacy of a thousand dollars to go for a year to the De Mille Ladies

College at Whitby. It was a somewhat unusual adventure for a country-bred Ontario girl in the early 1890's, and the taste and skill which she acquired as a result in drawing and painting was a still more unusual accomplishment. It set her off a little from her rosy-cheeked, coarse-fingered girlish companions. It gave her—and the country boys around were quick to realize the fact—just a bit of distinction.

Yet her real distinction lay much deeper. Her alert, direct, faintly appraising gaze bespoke intelligence and character. She formed her own opinions and made her own judgments; and there was a refreshing, slightly astringent candour in the way she spoke her mind. When she got back from the Ladies College in 1893, there were at least four or five young men who were eager enough to claim her hand in marriage; but she made her choice coolly and deliberately, and for the shrewd reasons which had guided the Vicar of Wakefield in his selection of a mate. William Anson was an Innis, and the Innises, ever since the conversion of old Samuel, were known to be strict Baptists, with the highest reputation for temperance, probity, and hard-work; and honest sobriety, in an age when so many young careers were wrecked through drunkenness, was an asset highly to be prized. Mary did not hesitate very long. She chose William Innis. She came to live, for the first few months of her married life, at the old Innis place on the tenth concession. But she had no intention of waiting tamely until Samuel died and her husband might inherit the family homestead. She wanted her own life. She wanted to begin it at once. And it was largely because of her insistence that the next move was made, and made so soon.

By that time, of course, there was no more crown land to be acquired simply by the payment of the patent fees. Farms in Oxford County had to be bought; but the Innises, though far

6

from affluent, had prospered reasonably, and old Samuel Innis, who was to die four years later, was able, as one of the last important acts of his career, to set his son William up as an independent farmer. The hundred-acre farm to the north, fronting on the eighth concession, was purchased from John Singer; and after paying the purchase price of three thousand five hundred dollars, Samuel Innis turned the property over, encumbered only by a mortgage of fifteen hundred dollars, to his son. Obviously William started his career under conditions very different from those which had confronted his pioneer ancestors. The back-breaking labour of clearing his farm had already been done, and its two previous occupants had left primitive buildings. But here again William and Mary decided to start anew. They determined to build a third house, further north and below the crest of the ridge, but still a fair distance from the concession road. It was a simple rectangular structure, built of boards and scantling, lath and plaster, with two storeys and three small rooms on each. For a time a mason and a carpenter were employed at the princely wage of three dollars a day; during most of the summer William busied himself superintending or aiding the construction; and by autumn the little house was ready for occupation. It was done, and done just in time, for Mary was already getting close to her confinement; and on November 5, 1894, her eldest child, Harold Adams Innis, was born.

Harold began life, protected and unaware, among conditions which were harsh and exacting and laborious. Every day during the first winter his mother trudged south to the old Innis farm to get fresh milk, for they had no cow. The first crops of wheat and rye were sown broadcast by hand in the ancient fashion, for there was no drill. In those early days, the one great source of cash income was the contract for hauling milk from the farms along a route of several miles eastward to the cheese factory at Bookton. Every day Mary Innis washed eight or ten great milk cans in preparation for the next day's run; and all through the year she strove by every means in her power—raising poultry, growing vegetables, drying apples on her ever-busy stove—to increase the small output of the farm and to reduce its inevitable dependence upon the local village store at Hawtrey. The long commercial slump, which had lasted with few and brief interruptions from 1874, still stifled the pent energies of Canada during these first years of the new Innis enterprise. William and Mary were not aware that they were approaching the end of that economic enormity, the "Great Depression" of the last quarter of the nineteenth century. They knew at first that times were very hard. They began gradually to realize that conditions were improving. They had, in fact, entered upon a new phase of their own, and their country's, history. A fundamental change of circumstances occurred. At long last Canada entered upon a great period of national expansion.

Slowly, the farm's character began to alter. Wheat, which had been an important cash crop in the district for generations, declined gradually in importance as the great prairies of the new Canadian West were exploited and as southern Ontario grew more industrialized. William had always shown an interest in animals and a sympathetic care in their handling; and he now moved forward to take his small part in supplying the need of a new and much more urbanized community. The number of his horses, cattle, and pigs was steadily increased; the fields were now largely sown with the turnips, mangels, and corn which would properly support the farm's livestock and its expanding dairying activities. Slowly, unpretentiously, the enterprise succeeded; and at last, in the

8

enlargement and improvement of the small house near the crest of the ridge, there came an open announcement of modest prosperity. The first frame rectangle was faced with brick; and a second rectangle, slightly larger than the original and also made of brick, was built out at right angles towards the west. The accommodation of the house was almost doubled, yet for need as well as for comfort. William and Mary's small family was growing and in the end there were four children, Harold, Lillian, Hughena, and Samuel.

In the meantime, Harold had ceased to be a baby and was becoming a small boy. As soon as he could watch and listen he became aware of the farm's manifold demands and benefactions. As soon as he could toddle across the barnyard, he was quick to notice the recurring succession of its activities. The rhythm of the farm danced slowly along his blood, echoed faintly in his memory ever afterwards. He came to know the land, its contours, soils and vegetation, with a curiously intimate, even affectionate, particularity. He could tell by a glance at a particular chestnut or hickory nut what tree it had come from; he could almost infallibly identify the source of a bucket of maple sap by its distinctive flavour. The mammoth operations of the farm pursued their course above his head and in majestic indifference to his small presence; but he was always there, interested, round-eyed, untalkative, noting every detail of their operations. In the first pale fine days of early March, he foraged about for bits of firewood, while the maple sap bubbled lusciously in the great iron kettle. He carried pitchers of cooling drinks to the men toiling away in the dried yellow fields under the scorching suns of August; and, on dark afternoons in late December, he sat at the table in the farm-house kitchen, plucking the fowls that were to be carried in next day to the Christmas market at Brantford. His alert, direct gaze—the gaze of his mother—was upon everything. He noted similarities, he detected differences; he was conscious of both recurrence and change. And gradually the farm became known to him through an incredible mass of detail which was regarded, not in isolation, but as part of a vast organic whole.

The century drew towards its close. He was five years old now. On Sundays he was taken regularly for religious instruction to the austere red-brick Baptist Church in Otterville; and he kept begging his mother for permission to go to public school. One autumn day she walked with him down the farm lane to the road and put him in charge of one of the big girls of the neighbourhood who was on her way to school. Harold started off down the road, looked back, saw his mother waving encouragement to him in his new venture, and plodded bravely forward. It was not a long or tiring walk, for School Section No. 1 South Norwich was established at a conveniently close distance, only about a half a mile away on the eighth concession road. The school—it was a typical small rural Ontario school— had one fair-sized room which was crowded with a large number of children of all ages, of distinctly varying abilities, and at quite different levels of training. The instruction of this full hierarchy of public school classes was a highly complex business which exhausted the ingenuity of the teacher and at the same time encouraged and assisted the brighter pupils. A clever pupil was not necessarily restricted to the work of his own class and compelled to travel forward at the rate of its slowest member. When his own assigned lesson was finished, he could follow with interest what was going on in the form above him; and if—which was not too difficult in such circumstances—he could show an ability to follow it successfully, then rapid promotion was fairly easy.

Harold passed with fair rapidity through S. S. No. 1 South

Norwich. He took advantage of the opportunities of its single schoolroom. He did very well, but he was not unduly conscious of superiority; and it was with something of a shock that, on one occasion, he emerged the victor in a spelling contest in which most of the contestants were considerably older than himself. He was a little surprised also, as his schooldays drew towards their close, to realize that his parents were considering the continuation of his education, and obviously nursing the hope that his career would be very different from that of a farmer. His father suggested that he should try to become a teacher. His mother may already have been secretly looking forward to the proud day when her earnest, clever son would become a clergyman. She said little, but he sensed that she was ambitious for his future.

The plan of continuing Harold's education may originally have been hers. She and William had probably been considering it for some time already. And, late in Harold's school career, an event occurred which may have helped them to reach a firm decision. In 1905, their fourth child, called Samuel after his grandfather, was born. They now had a family of two sons and two daughters. The maintenance of the farm and its continuance inside the connection were assured. A child could be spared for a very different vocation and their choice was virtually made. Harold was a boy who promised well, and he now fulfilled the first modest instalment of their expectations. In the spring of 1905, he successfully passed the provincial public examination, called the "entrance" examination, which qualified pupils for admission to the secondary schools. The next phase of his career was settled.

In the autumn, he entered Otterville High School. The little public school down the concession road had seemed a simple, approachable, even friendly building. But Otterville, the principal small town of the district, was more than two miles away to the west; and although he was very familiar with the chill, austerely simple interior of its Baptist Church, the Otterville High School was an unknown and formidable institution. It drew its pupils from both town and countryside for miles around. It had an impressive record in sports; and a country boy like Harold, who had no money to spend on equipment and little opportunity of acquiring skill in games, was very conscious of his unhappy disadvantage. He had no comparable difficulty, however, with his school work. Day after day, helped on by an occasional lift in a waggon or a sleigh, he trudged the long miles back and forth to the high school; and when the summer of 1907 finally came he had proved, by an ample demonstration, that he was fully worthy of a secondary-school education.

He had also come to the end of the resources of the Otterville High School. That imposing institution, for all its sporting spirit and its successful hockey teams, was discovered to have a serious limitation. It was a continuation school not a collegiate institute. It began but could not complete a secondary-school education; and if Harold was to get all that a secondary-school education had to offer, it was obvious that he would have to go to the Collegiate Institute in Woodstock. Woodstock! If the thought of Otterville had awakened some qualms, the prospect of the transfer to Woodstock was positively intimidating. Woodstock was a large town, full of dangers and seductions. It was twenty miles away; it could be reached only by railway; and attendance at its high school could mean nothing less than two train journeys every single day of the school year. These small apprehensions, these nervous agitations were natural enough; but they dashed themselves in vain against the solid decision which William and Mary had already taken. Harold had deserved the Woodstock High School. He would go to the Woodstock High School. And one bright golden morning in early September, he took his place in the seven o'clock train. The passenger coach was full of young people, most of whom were entirely strange to him. He sat on the red plush seat—a tall, awkward, gangling youth, with dark unruly hair and a sensitive mobile face—feeling embarrassed and forlorn. He considered the future with anxiety yet with determination. And then the train started with a jerk and clanked slowly out of the station towards the north.

II

Woodstock Collegiate Institute—a red-brick, two-storey building of what must have seemed, to Harold, magnificent dimensions—stood on Riddell Street, about a mile away from the Grand Trunk Railway station. It was the typical high school, of a typical southern Ontario town, in the days before the great development of technical and occupational instruction. There was a principal, I. M. Levan, and perhaps half-a-dozen teachers—Patterson, the mathematician, Cole, the natural science master, and W. J. Salter, who taught Latin. They were all good teachers, capable of communicating the interest and excitement of their subjects; and Cole in particular was an enthusiast who could inspire his pupils to collect specimens and keep nature diaries. The classes were not too large. The masters had an opportunity of getting to know something of their pupils; and Levan came to watch the onward progress of the awkward country boy from Otterville with almost affectionate interest.

For four years Harold went to the Woodstock High School. It was, in many ways, a hard, exacting experience. He had to get up in time to catch the Grand Trunk Railway train which left Otterville for Woodstock every morning at seven o'clock. It was a typical short local train—an informal, sociable, friendly train, which rattled onward in a comfortable, unhurried fashion, taking its own time, yet always keeping reasonably close to schedule. At every stop along the way to Woodstock it took on a few high school pupils; it carried them all back again at night to their respective destinations; and even on the dullest days, the laughter and chatter of the children made the journey something of an excursion. Once in a while, but only at very great intervals, an event of stupendous and dramatic importance occurred which interrupted this placid and monotonous routine. On one occasion, a heavy freight, travelling immediately in front of the school train, crashed off the track at the bottom of the hill going out from Burgessville; and once—a still more exciting and memorable episode—a heavy snow storm blocked the line completely and the Grand Trunk Railway put up the entire school population of their late afternoon local at an hotel in Woodstock.

But these glorious experiences were few and very far between. On almost all occasions the journey from Otterville to Woodstock and back was completely uneventful. It was also monotonous, time-consuming, and very tiring. There was a walk of two miles from the Innis farm to the Otterville railway station; there was another walk of a mile from the Woodstock railway station to the Woodstock High School. It was six miles to go in all; and every day, in every week of every month, in all weathers and temperatures, the journey had to be performed. He had to rush away from the farm in the morning; he had to leave the school in a hurry at night; and by the time he got home and had swallowed his dinner, the evening was already far advanced. There was never enough time for study at night; there was not much opportunity for participation in the sports or other activities which went on outside the classroom at Woodstock. He was in the school, but not completely of it. He knew little of its recreations or associations. He made relatively few friends; and Hubert Kemp, who was a year or two ahead of him, was one of the few Woodstock boys who greeted him kindly. During all these years, he remained the country boy, poor, awkward, ill-at-ease, yet earnest and determined.

From the beginning he knew that he must succeed. He could not admit the possibility of failure. There was too much at stake. His parents, in paying his fees and in providing him with clothes and railway fares, were something, though perhaps not a great deal, out of pocket. They had sacrificed more in foregoing his help about the farm; and he himself, in the daily journey to and from Woodstock, had put an enormous amount of time and exertion into the business of getting an education. All this effort must not be made in vain; he must try his best to justify it; and he put every ounce of his ability and energy into the struggle. He was a good student, usually well above average, though not consistently brilliant. During his first year at the school, he obtained an average of about 76 per cent.; and in 1911 he passed his lower school examinations with honours. "Accept my heartiest congratulations on your well-deserved success," Principal Levan wrote him on August 15, "I am very proud of you and I hope to have you back in the Fourth Form next year."

That autumn, as Principal Levan had hoped, he entered the Fourth Form. He had spent three years at Woodstock Collegiate Institute; and now—as always—he was in a hurry. He had done reasonably well in the past; and he determined to put his ability and energy to the test of a supreme achievement. The goal, to which his father had pointed years before, was still his objective. He wanted to be a teacher. But he had still to fit himself for his professional training at the Normal School. The work prescribed for admission to the Normal School was a two-years' course; and the public examination came in two parts, one at the end of each year, like Junior and Senior Matriculation. He determined to take the two-years' course in one and to try both parts of the public examination at the end of the next session. It was a bold decision and yet perhaps not so unusual as it would have been later, when school curricula had become more inflexible, and individual enterprise less respected.

He had to master a staggering range of subjects. He was working at top speed and under the greatest possible disadvantage. All autumn and winter he struggled under his appalling burden; and when summer arrived and the examination drew closer, he moved into Woodstock to the house of a relative in order to gain as much time as possible and to minimize the risks of the ordeal which he faced. He began the examination; and then, with ill-fated and dismaying suddenness, he began to feel out of sorts. He had, though he did not realize it, contracted a case of German measles. He did not know that he was ill. He only knew that he felt miserable, but that somehow or other, whatever his physical state might be, he must continue the examination. There was no other possible course; and there was only one faint ray of hope in the black tragedy of his situation. The next day was a free day. No examination was scheduled. There were twenty-four hours in which to effect a recovery. He went to bed with his books, read a little, slept a lot, perspired copiously, felt acutely unhappy, and next day, pale, shaky but resolute, arose to continue the examination. He may not have been very confident, but he passed. He probably did not do very well, for, in such circumstances, only a very precocious person could have done very well; but he was through both parts of the examination at a single try.

Teaching—primary or secondary school teaching—was apparently his goal. He was within sight of it now. And if he had entered at once upon the obvious next stage of his career, he would have gone off to begin a teacher's professional training. He did not do it. Such professional training could be obtained at only a few places in the province, each some distance from Otterville. It was impossible for him to commute each day to London or Toronto, as he had done to Woodstock. He would have to go to a city where there was a Normal School, and, for months, pay all the expenses of fees and books and board and lodging. It would cost money—more money that his parents could probably afford, more than he would dream of requesting of them. And he decided gloomily that until he discovered some way of earning a substantial lump of cash, the next stage of education would have inevitably to be postponed. It was true that already, while he had been attending school in Woodstock, he had found means of earning small sums of money. He had trapped muskrats and sold their pelts; he had worked on Saturdays in his uncle's general store at Hawtrey. But obviously these amounts—magnificent as they had seemed at the moment—were totally inadequate for his new purpose. He must have a job.

At this point his father, who was one of the trustees for School Section No. 1 of South Norwich, approached him with a suggestion. School Section No. 1 needed a teacher. And until a suitable teacher with a permanent certificate could be found, why should not Harold undertake the job? In a short while, this unexceptionable piece of family patronage was arranged. He had his father's support and the other

17

trustee's agreement and he was backed up by a strong, and significantly worded recommendation from the faithful Mr. Levan of Woodstock Collegiate. "He is a splendid worker," the principal wrote, "and is not afraid to undertake any task, however difficult. He is, moreover, a young man of excellent character, and can be relied upon to do his best under all circumstances."

It was not easy to return as a teacher to the school in which he had finished his career as a pupil only a few years before. He could hardly bring himself to stand up before his own brother, the brothers and sisters of his old comrades, and even some of his younger fellow pupils themselves. Somehow, by a violent effort of will, he mastered his sensitivity; and after the first walk to the school and the first few awful moments on the schoolroom platform, he felt ready enough to cope with the problems of his new job. Yet they were not easy. He quickly came to see how much patience, sympathetic understanding, and planning ability were required of a country school teacher. The complex arrangement of instructions, assignments, and recitations for pupils of all ages and classes, from which he had profited so much as a boy, now depended upon his own foresight and ingenuity. He tried to assist bright boys. He coped with difficult and refractory children. He soothed irate parents, who occasionally, at the instigation of their sons and daughters, descended in a rage upon the schoolhouse. He saw the first term through not unsuccessfully. And then, as was to be expected of a school board which took its duties seriously, another qualified master with a permanent certificate was secured. And, at Christmas of the year 1912, Harold's career as a public-school teacher came to an end.

He did not greatly regret the fact. Perhaps the most important aspect of this brief period of teaching was the part that it played in his own education. The professional future which his father had described so enviously a few years before no longer seemed so attractive to him. He looked speculatively, and with diminishing enthusiasm, at the prospect of a lifetime spent in a small country school in a rural township such as South Norwich. The years during which he had commuted to Woodstock had been hard and exacting; but they had certainly given him a strong relish for the world that lay beyond the Otterville railway station. The farm— and the tight, strict Baptist community of which he was a part—had made him. The farm had given him his instinct for simplicity, his capacity for continuous hard work, his fund of rather cynical down-to-earth common sense, and his ability to communicate understandingly with people in a wide variety of walks of life. The strict sense of values and the feeling of devotion to a cause, which became so characteristic of him in later life, were derived, in part at least, from the instruction imparted so zealously and unquestioningly inside the severely unadorned walls of the Baptist Church at Otterville. He was developing a great belief in the value of personality—in his own worth— and a great impatience with organizations, hierarchies, dignities, and rules. This was, in fact, his basic moral and spiritual equipment. He would carry it through life. And South Norwich had given it to him.

But South Norwich had nearly finished its work. It had given him all it had to give. He began to feel that he had exhausted most of the possibilities of the eighth concession road, and the schoolhouse, and his uncle's shop at Hawtrey, and the chill interior of the red-brick Baptist Church at Otterville. For years, ever since he could remember, he had gone regularly, with his deeply religious parents, to the Baptist services; and so long as his childhood and boyhood lasted, all that was really required of him was faithful attendance at church and Sunday school and conduct in accordance with the rigid moral code which they imparted. But now this period was drawing to a close. He was aware of an ominously approaching change. The church of his parents emphasized adult baptism as the central part of its creed; and baptism must, of course, be preceded by a deliberate public testimony of faith. He was a young man now—he had turned eighteen. He sensed that from now on the pressure of the community, overt and concealed, upon him would probably increase in intensity.

During the last months of the winter of 1912–13, he helped in the easy off-season work of the farm and carefully considered his future. With a very small part of his fabulous earnings as a teacher, he made himself two presents. He purchased a ferret and tramped the woodlots of the ninth concession, hunting and catching live woodchucks, muskrats, and rabbits. He purchased a subscription—no large metropolitan newspaper had yet entered the farmhouse—to the Toronto *Globe*; and he devoured its long, detailed accounts of the incredibly protracted debates which followed the introduction of Sir Robert Borden's Naval Aid Bill in the autumn of 1912. Harold's father was a Liberal, a devoted follower of Sir Wilfrid Laurier. Any other paper but the *Globe* was quite unthinkable! And, as often before in rural Liberal households, the *Globe* exercised a distinct educational influence. It gave Harold a respectful admiration for the range of Sir Wilfrid's vocabulary. It sent him scurrying to the dictionary to look up words. Above all, it strengthened his interest in the outside world— in Canada and its national affairs. By the time spring came, he had made up his mind about this own future. He would not begin the professional training required of a teacher immediately. He would go instead to a university—not, indeed, to a secular institution such as the University of Toronto or the University of Western Ontario, but to McMaster University which had been established in Toronto for just such carefully brought up sons of Baptist parents as himself.

Years before, when he had first travelled on the early morning train to Woodstock, he had noted a small circumstance which had stirred him curiously. At Norwich Junction, the Otterville train met the train from Tillsonburg which swept on grandly towards Brantford and the east; and every morning the trainman, in his droning voice, called out the evocative names of the eastern cities, ending with Toronto, which Harold had never seen. He was going to Toronto now himself. He would probably be there for the better part of three years. He would come back, of course; but he felt obscurely it would be for shorter and shorter periods. And in any case it would be a new and different Harold who would return. The first phase of his existence was definitely over.

III

Toronto was the biggest city in the province, and McMaster University, though fairly small, was a thriving institution. Everything promised well. The next phase of his existence ought to have opened interestingly, excitingly; but it did not. Within a few weeks he was feeling both lonely and disillusioned. He had, in fact, out of ignorance and over-confidence, made two important errors in judgment. He had assumed that the seemingly enormous earnings of his half year of teaching would go a long way towards paying his expenses in Toronto; and he had somehow taken it for granted that entering, as an Honour Matriculation student, into the second year of university would not make a great deal of difference in his university career. On both counts he was wrong. As soon as he had paid his fees and rented a room at the staggering rate of a dollar and fifty cents a week, he realized just how pitifully inadequate his resources were. He began to practise rigid economies; and the virtual food rationing which he imposed upon himself caused him rapidly to lose weight. The depression of his spirits had, in part, a physical origin; but the unexpected loneliness which he felt, even in the midst of groups and coteries and crowds, was probably the main source of his persistent dejection. A new student, fresh to the University, he had entered the second year at a time when his year's associations and friendships were already largely made. If he had been able to live in college, he might have broken through this isolation quickly enough; but he was stuck off in his solitary room in a boarding-house. He felt terribly alone. He haunted the library and tried to make the most out of the place; but it was no good. By the time the term ended and he went back to Otterville for the Christmas holidays, he had reached the gloomy decision that he would not return.

As soon as his mother saw him, she knew what had happened. The crisis in her plans for her son was at hand. He was, she felt instinctively, making a fatal, an irremediable mistake. She would do all she could to prevent the commission of this catastrophic error. But she realized intuitively that her son would be convinced only by a kind of knowledge which she did not possess and a type of argument of which she was incapable. She must have help, and at once; and to her knowledge there was only one source from which help could come. Her brother William, who had begun his medical training at the University of Western Ontario at a later age than was usual, would surely appreciate the value of higher education, and would help to keep Harold from his folly. She wrote to her brother, begging him to come to Otterville to discuss her son's future, even offering him money for this special journey;

and a few days later, before the Christmas season ended, William arrived. He was fresh from his own studies; he had won his way to them with difficulty; and he flung himself with conviction into what was perhaps the crucial battle of his nephew's career. In the end, Harold was overborne. His pride—for his intellect had never really been engaged—yielded to the weight of this combined persuasion. He consented to accept as much financial help as his parents could give him. He agreed to go back and finish his year at McMaster.

The next term—the winter term of 1914—was distinctly better. Though in January he had to report a failure in Latin, he was much more satisfied, on the whole, with his academic progress. He salved his conscience during the long vacation by putting in a steady, arduous summer's work on the farm. And despite the war, which broke out that August, and the unsettlement which it immediately began to produce, he returned to McMaster in the autumn in a far more equable and eager frame of mind than he would have believed possible eight months before. The ground was more familiar now, and he found his way with ease. He became more fully aware of the range of opportunities which the University had to offer. He began to appreciate the nature of the different subjects, and the approaches and styles of the different professors. The older men—McLay in English and Ten Broeke in philosophy—brought liberal enlightenment to a young man who had been brought up in too much fundamentalist dogma and too little English literature. But in the main, as Harold began to discover preferences and make choices, his interest centred on different subjects and younger men. He was devoted to W. S. Wallace, the young lecturer in history, who had just returned from Oxford; and he was extremely impressed by W. J. Donald, who assisted the Chancellor, A. L.

McCrimmon, in teaching the social sciences and who did a good deal of the lecturing in political economy.

He had come to the University with the vague expectation of becoming a lawyer. A lawyer, he assumed, would have to be a barrister and a barrister must, of necessity, be trained in the arts of public speaking. Even in the autumn of 1913, during the weeks of his most acute misery, he had pored over books on "oratory"; and now, with reviving spirits and returning self-confidence, he mustered sufficient courage to take part in the discussions of the University debating society. As soon as he was on his feet, he found that he began to enjoy the experience. He did not do badly. At the next opportunity, he spoke again. He went on attending the debates. He ended up by winning the annual "oratorical" contest and being elected president of the debating society. It was his first real public triumph among his fellow-students. And it was also the year of his first great academic success. At the examinations in the spring of 1915 he obtained first class standing in history. He won a prize in philosophy and the D. E. Thomson scholarship in his favourite subject, political economy.

He had begun to realize his power. He felt enormously encouraged. Within a little over a year, his whole outlook on life had completely altered. He knew that he had mastered the University; he began to feel that he was ready for another vigorous attempt to solve the financial problem of his education. He hoped again to relieve his parents of part of their burden; he wanted to complete the recovery of his own sense of independence; and, by great good fortune, the kind of opportunity for which he was trained and ready lay open before him. The new prairie West, with its young pioneering families and crowds of small children, was clamouring for primary school teachers; and since, because of transport difficulties in winter time, the great majority of western rural schools held their sessions during the summer, the young college students of the east found it possible to respond to this demand. Along with two or three other McMaster students, Harold decided that he would go west that summer to teach. In some fashion, he discovered the name of Andrew Semple, who was chairman of the school board at a little place called Landonville, near Vermilion in northern Alberta. He wrote to Semple, enclosing his credentials; and in short order he found himself virtually engaged to teach at the new "Northern Star" school for five months at a salary of seven hundred and twenty dollars. Up to the last minute, his professional status was uncertain. Despite his experience in Ontario, he was still not sure that he could obtain a temporary certificate from the Alberta Department of Education. But after some inquiries he decided that this was a calculated risk that it would be reasonable to take. On the last day of April, he set out for the West.

It was his first great journey into new lands and among strange people. He travelled direct. There was no farewell visit to Otterville. And very early on the fourth morning after his departure from Toronto, he stepped off the train on the deserted station platform of the small town of Vermilion. The journey by stage to Landonville, at a breakneck speed over forty miles of abominable roads, was a novel and exciting experience; and the realization that from there on the normal and accepted method of travelling anywhere was by horseback came as a distinct but not unpleasant surprise. Semple was one of the district's most successful farmers, and he and his wife and household gave Harold a heart-warming, typically western welcome. He gladly accepted an invitation to stay and board with them; and that night, as he lay in his small room in their poplar-log house, he could hear the coyotes howling forlornly in the distance. The very next day he began teaching at the Northern Star School. It was a tiny, neat box-like structure, painted white, which was planted incongrously in the middle of the rough, unbroken prairie with a thick poplar wood beyond.

He stayed at Landonville until the autumn. The district was an English-speaking one, and he encountered no language difficulties at the Northern Star; but the majority of his twelve or fifteen pupils were children of rather shiftless immigrants, and their mediocre abilities did not greatly inspire him. He found a great deal more interest in the activities of the Semples, and of their principal friends, the Stanleys, and in the strenuous work and play of the pioneer community around him. In contrast with the diversified and complex agriculture of southern Ontario, farming around Landonville, in northern Alberta, seemed a relatively simple affair. The main business of the district was the growing of grain; and, as soon as the crop ripened in late August and early September, the whole community flung itself, with passionate concentration, into the task of harvesting. Everybody worked furiously then. Everybody seemed, to Harold, to play with equally tireless energy in the long, relatively easy interval between sowing and reaping. There was fishing and riding and hunting, and, on great occasions such as the first of July, horse-racing and bronco-busting. There were picnics among the lakes to the north, and dances in the schoolhouse, which went on until two and three o'clock in the morning. Nobody paid the slightest attention to time. Nobody had the faintest concern for distance. People were always starting off, at apparently any hour of the day or night, on what seemed stupendous journeys; and those who shirked these enterprises and failed to return these visits, were invariably regarded with mild contempt.

On the morning of September 11, when he first looked out of his window in the Semples' house, he discovered that there were two or three inches of snow upon the ground. The season was closing in the final struggle of threshing; but he stayed out the full five months which his contract had stipulated, and it was not until the beginning of October that he started east for McMaster University. He had had a most rewarding experience. He had travelled three-quarters of the way across the continent and had exchanged the placid, well-kept fields of southern Ontario for the rolling, half-broken, wooded parklands of northern Alberta. He had made the acquaintance of the new West. He had learned something of the West's peculiar problems. The anxieties and vexations of high interest-rates and transport problems had become familiar to him through very real examples. He brought back with him some understanding of the West's conception of its own nature, and of its attitude to the nation as a whole.

He came back with something else as well. He was conscious of a growing preoccupation with the war, and its course and consequences. Even in such a remote district as Landonville, which he had possibly assumed would be relatively unaffected, the impact of the war was obvious and increasingly heavy. A few young men had enlisted; recruiting agents were about; and already there was talk of conscription. When he got back to Toronto early in October, the whole atmosphere seemed noticeably more tense and determined than it had been only five months before. He decided that he would not commit himself yet, partly because he knew that his parents were terrified by the mere thought of his enlistment, but mainly because he had determined that, if possible, he was going to complete his university career.

Despite these worries, he came back with enthusiasm for his final year at McMaster. He had money in his pocket, as a result of his long hard summer's work. He joined a co-operative dining club in which the members did the culinary work themselves; and the worst of his financial difficulties was really over. His position in the University was now assured; and, as the work of his course progressed, he came to realize his own special interests and abilities more fully. He tucked away in his mind a statement of his history lecturer, W. S. Wallace, to the effect that the economic interpretation of history was not the only interpretation of history but was the deepest. His own interest in the detail of economic phenomena and in the broad lines of economic development was growing rapidly. Academically he was specializing as much as possible in history and political economy; and in the debating society his favourite questions were economic in character. The most important debate of his academic career was the intercollegiate debate between McMaster University and Trinity College, held on December 3, 1915. The question at issue was "that commercial prosperity is necessarily a cause of war". Harold's associate from McMaster was J. W. Davis; his opponents from Trinity were R. F. Palmer and G. F. Kingston, the future Primate of Canada. For weeks he put all his ability and energy into the preparations for this contest. His main theme was that the interrelations of commerce had created an interdependent world. "Commercial prosperity," he concluded his speech, "is not necessarily the cause of war; it is the only panacea for peace."

This triumph—for McMaster won the debate, though not by a unanimous decision of the judges—was the last great achievement of the old pre-war kind in Harold's college career. From then on, the war, which was now dominating the entire economic and social life of the country, began to have an increasingly disruptive effect on Canadian universities. The appalling mass slaughter on the fighting fronts of Western Europe forced every allied government into a relentless search for men. At the beginning of 1916, Sir Robert Borden announced that the objective of the Canadian army was five hundred thousand soldiers; and during the next few months great numbers of senior students in Canadian universities volunteered for active service. At McMaster, as at other institutions, their departure was eased by the granting of their degrees without examination; and late in March, fifteen of Harold's friends and acquaintances left the University without completing the academic year. Suddenly the place seemed vacant and desolate. The fag-end of the term had become almost meaningless. But Harold decided firmly that he would not avail himself of the dubious gift of an easy degree. Whether he enlisted or not, he would stay on until the end of the term, write his examinations, and finish his university course in the normal way.

Yet what was he to do then? Should he enlist? Slowly he groped his way towards his own independent decision. But, in the meantime, his family and his close friends, who had their own conception of his character and future, urged a very different course of action upon him. They believed that his duty lay in Canada, as a clergyman of the Baptist Church. There were difficulties, of course. Harold had not yet made public profession of faith and received baptism. The pressure upon him to do so had been growing steadily ever since he had reached his majority in the previous autumn; but so far he had not complied with the appeals of those who were closest to him. This was regrettable; but a reluctance to undergo the public formality of a profession of faith was not uncommon in sensitive young people; and in Harold's case, and in a time of national crisis, was such a profession really necessary? His known Christian character and conduct could speak for him alone. His high sense of purpose, as well as his scholarly ability, marked him out as the person most suited to take over the duties of the less devoted and less gifted people who were called away to battle. To Harold's friends and relatives, the argument seemed irrefutable. Quickly they put him in touch with a group of Baptists near Kemptville who were eager to have him take over the charge of the South Gower church. The arrangements were virtually complete. The fact that Harold was not yet a church member was tacitly disregarded. Even the most conservative church leaders smiled a benevolent approval.

Then, at the last moment, Harold drew back. His long mental conflict was over. He had decided to enlist. He had held back so long in large measure out of consideration of his family's feelings. But he saw now that he could yield no longer to their fears and entreaties, and he was unwilling to become a passive instrument in the plans of his friends. He had made up his own mind; but his decision, though it was in part a declaration of independence, was at the same time solidly based on the Christian principles to which he and his family and friends instinctively appealed. For him the war was quite simply a great moral issue; and he could not see that, as a Christian, he could possibly avoid taking his share in its determination. He had been brought up in a Christian home by parents who were devout members of an austerely evangelical communion; he had gone to a university which provided a liberal education in an accordance with the Christian principles which this communion professed; and although he had not yet made the open and mature avowal of his faith which the Baptist Church required, there could be no doubt that he implicitly accepted its teachings and tried instinctively to follow its guidance. Germany, as he saw it, had begun the war by breaking a treaty, violating its word, and running rampant at the expense of other and weaker nations; and if Germany went unpunished, it would mean the end of the Christian hope for the world. "If I had no faith in Christianity," he told his sister, "I don't think I would go."

Early in May he took his degree at Convocation, went back to Otterville for a brief visit at the farm, and returned to Toronto to join the 69th Battery at the Armories on University Avenue. There were only a few brief weeks of drilling when the news came that he was to join a draft proceeding immediately overseas; and he was given a last leave to go home to see his people. He walked out proudly from Otterville Station towards the farm. His mind was settled. He felt physically very fit; and he was in all the glory of his new uniform. He had devised an innocent strategem in order to surprise his mother; and instead of walking along the open road and up the long lane to the house, which would inevitably have given his approach away, he struck out across the fields and past the buildings of the neighbouring farms. It was a hot bright summer day and he felt warm and excited. He was twenty-one years of age, a tall slight young man, with a long steady stride. And his thin mobile face, with its sensitive humorous mouth, was alight with expectation.

IV

The war was the second great influence in his life. The farm had formed his character. The war of 1914–18 tested it in what was probably the most terrible ordeal which the English-speaking peoples have so far experienced in the twentieth century. Up to that time, Harold had led a very sheltered and restricted life. He had been born into a simple, rural, severely Puritan family; he had given his youth and young manhood to the peaceful, traditional pursuits of study and hard farm labour. And now, with little preparation and with almost no appreciation of what was involved, he was suddenly caught up in a life of fast movement, and violent activity, and deadly peril.

The pace of events was unprecedentedly swift. On July 13, a day of terrific heat with vast milling crowds at the Union Station in Toronto, he left on the troop train for Montreal. Before the end of July he was established in Shorncliffe camp, near Folkestone, in Kent, overlooking the English Channel. Three months' time was sufficient for him to take all the courses and to pass all the tests in signalling and gunnery; and early in November he was off to Glasgow, Edinburgh, and Inverness, on a six-day leave which he knew very well was the immediate prelude to his transfer to France. Before the end of the month a packed troop train carried him down to Southampton; and a few hours later he walked up the long flight of steps to the quay at Le Havre. There was a stop of only two or three days at the base in France; and then, one cool December night, under a dark sky blazing with stars, the chaplain gave the troops a last earnest address, and the pipe band played gaily as they marched past and away to the trains which were to carry them to the front.

Long months before, when the question of his enlistment was solemnly discussed, he had tried to convince his family of the wisdom of the step he intended taking by every kind of argument and assurance. Joining the army, he told his father and mother, would be a profitable investment. He could travel and see the world. And if he volunteered in time, instead of waiting until he was drafted by conscription, he would be able to make his own choice among the various branches of the service. The infantry, he informed his sister, was "no place for a man if he wants to come back alive"; but both the artillery and the signallers were safe jobs "and a long way back from the firing line". In the next few months he was to put these confident generalizations to a pitiless test; and he discovered immediately that the sharp distinctions he had been making were almost completely invalid. There were no easy preliminaries; there was no long period of probation. Quickly he was moved to the 4th Battery of the First Brigade of the First Division of the Canadian Expeditionary Force; and he plunged at once into that state of prolonged, immobile discomfort varied only by periods of violent slaughter which was the common portion of all the fighting forces on the western front. The weather in north-eastern France during those winter months seemed to alternate between pouring rain and damp, biting cold with harsh winds. There was mud everywhere: "the only way this country could be muddier," he told his mother, "would be to be bigger." He was dirty, tired, hungry, and cold a good part of the time.

He encountered front-line fighting for the first time when his unit was moved up to Bully Grenay, in the Lens region. He learnt his job as a signaller in comparatively easy circumstances, for the area about Bully Grenay was at that time fairly peaceful. He did not stay there long. He was moved again—a move of great significance—back to Camblain Chatelain, known with wry affection by the troops as "Charlie Chaplin"; and from then on, a single infinitesimal unit, he became involved in the vast laborious preparations for the Canadian attack on Vimy Ridge. From the middle of March the pace of events became ominously swifter. They had left

Camblain Chatelain and were working continuously up at the battery. New batteries were constantly arriving for what was obviously intended to be a tremendous attack. The shelling was now steady; there were frequent aeroplane fights in the sky; and all night long in mud and rain they toiled away, bringing up material behind the front line, in preparation for the advance of the artillery to new forward positions once the objectives of the attack had been gained.

On April 9, in the grey dawn of a spring morning, he waited just behind the Canadian line. The Ridge, which dominated the entire Lens-Arras landscape, rose mistily before him in slow, gradual, deceptively easy slopes. The sky was sombre. It was wet and bitterly cold; and a thin sleet, which thickened later into a heavy snowfall, was seeping drearily down. They waited anxiously in the tense unnatural silence; and then, at exactly half-past five o'clock, the whole long line of the Canadian guns, in appalling unison, opened up in the crashing eloquence of the barrage. For a time that seemed interminable, the world was filled with its hideous clamour. It would never end. And then, at long last, the barrage lifted; and the skyline ahead was filled with muddy-brown waves of Canadian infantry rolling slowly forward. The front-line German trench was taken; groups of German prisoners suddenly appeared; the wounded were stumbling back; there were dead everywhere; and all around the shells were bursting without cessation. The hours, which seemed both like minutes and like ages, went by. It was afternoon. The second and third lines of trenches were captured. The advance swept forward to the German batteries; and gradually the enemy's gunfire dwindled away to an occasional shell. The tension broke. There was almost silence. And the day drew slowly toward nightfall, and the snow came softly down.

34

For nearly three months the fighting about the Ridge continued. The Canadians only gradually consolidated their position; it was weeks before a new front line was firmly established; and Innis's battery was moved several times before it finally settled down below the Ridge and close to the town of Vimy itself. The Germans counter-attacked; there were periods of intense shelling; aeroplanes fought each other in the skies, and occasionally observation balloons moved slowly about far above them. But gradually, by very slow degrees, it began to be apparent that the excitement about the Ridge and Hill 70 was dying down. The rest periods were more frequent, there was more time for routine tasks. The strategists had, in fact, transferred their attention from Vimy to the muddy plains about Ypres; and only a little later the entire Canadian corps was to be moved north for the mass slaughter of Passchendaele.

On July 7—almost exactly three months after the first attack on Vimy Ridge—Innis and some of the other signallers of his battery started off to make their nightly observations from the old German gun-pits near the top of the Ridge. He might have evaded this particular trip. But he was weary of the endless repetitions of the routine of signalling and anxious to escape from them; and since one of the other men was missing, he agreed to do double duty. Slowly they worked their way up, along a slight elevation, towards the top of the ridge; and then, suddenly, a little distance behind, a German shell exploded. Innis looked back and, as the brief light of explosion flared, he saw an observation balloon hanging ominously in the sky. It was only too obvious what was happening. The balloon was in touch with a German battery and the two together were picking out groups of climbing Canadians wherever they could be found. Their own party had obviously been spotted. They began to hurry. And then the next shell fell in their midst.

Something thudded into his leg. He was knocked down. Blood began pouring out at his knee. And then, in the midst of his overwhelming weakness, he became aware that his companions had got out their Red Cross tackle and were binding up the wound. Somehow they carried him out of range of the observation balloon; somehow they got him down to the dressing station in an old chalk pit nearby. Dimly he was aware of their last congratulations on his successful "Blighty", of their departure, and of the long night on the stretcher in the dressing station. Then there was an ambulance, and a train, and then the long corridors and large rooms of something that must be a base hospital. He realized that they were preparing him for an operation which would remove the shell splinter from his leg. Unconsciousness overwhelmed him. Then he was awake again, lying on a bed in the hospital ward, waiting for orders as to his removal. And slowly he began to improve.

"It is just a week," he wrote to his mother on July 14, "since I got this comfortable little affair of mine." Within forty-eight hours he was on his way from Etaples to England; and at London, where he and the other wounded were taken out of the hospital train, long rows of welcoming women cast little gifts of flowers, and chocolate, and cigarettes upon their stretchers. At Endell Street Hospital in London trouble developed. A fresh operation was necessary to clean out the wound; but after this temporary set-back, he began slowly to improve again. Late in August he was put into a blue hospital suit and transferred to the Uxbridge Convalescent Home; and before the end of October he was moved again to the large Canadian General Hospital at Basingstoke. The massage and exercise which were prescribed for him did not seem to reduce the swelling in his leg; he walked laboriously and only with the aid of a stick; and the likelihood of his return to Canada grew greater and greater. In the meantime there were concerts, and movies and short excursions. He got a small job in the hospital post-office. And in January, when he felt much readier for walking and when his departure for Canada seemed imminent, he was given ten days' leave.

But for him these small occupations and diversions were not really important. His thoughts were already turning back to study. At Basingstoke there was ample time for reading; the Khaki College provided opportunites for work in such subjects as French grammar and shorthand; and—with a curious anticipation of the future—he entered, and won, a competition for an essay on "The Press". These small intellectual exercises took up the idle time and gave him some satisfaction; but what really interested him was a much more serious and formal course of study with a definite academic objective. For over six months now he had been making preparations for taking his M.A. at McMaster University. As far back as June 1917, in the brief lull in fighting which had preceded his serious injury on the Ridge at Vimy, he had written to his old University, asking for information about the requirements for the degree and proposing a thesis subject, "The Returned Soldier". Late in October, probably soon after he had been transferred to Basingstoke, he wrote again; and on both occasions it was D. A. MacGibbon who replied, giving helpful counsel about ways of collecting material for the thesis and methods of studying the set books. With this encouragement Innis plunged into the study of such great economic classics as Marshall's *Principles of Economics*. Once again he had a definite and congenial purpose.

The prospect of his immediate return to Canada gave point

and meaning to all these plans for the future. On February 21 —the long-awaited day of departure—he finally left Basingstoke for Liverpool. It was not until March 10 that the troops embarked in the huge ship *Vaterland*, with its covey of escorting destroyers; and there were eleven days of difficult travel through the wild March storms of the North Atlantic. At Quebec, on March 29, they waited expectantly while the familiar names—Toronto, Hamilton, London—of their various destinations were read out. Next morning, when Innis woke up, the train was standing in the station at Port Hope, and by noon they had arrived at London. The band played the usual reception tunes, the medical examination was quickly over; and late that afternoon, moving slowly and laboriously and with the aid of his inevitable stick, he climbed off the train at South Norwich and was clasped in his mother's arms. There was a great reception at the Town Hall in Otterville that evening, and over the next week the whole community, young and old, came crowding up to the farm at the top of Oak Ridge to welcome back the first of its returning sons.

In the meantime, Innis's thoughts had turned already to very different things. On Monday, April 1, two days only after his return to Otterville, he took the train to Toronto to consult with Dr. MacGibbon about his final preparation for the M.A. examination. His mind was busy with the future. He was torn between various possibilities and conflicting advice. But, despite these uncertainties, he realized very clearly that there were two essential preliminaries for any of the courses which he might pursue. He must demonstrate his ability once again, and in the face of obvious difficulties, by winning his M.A. degree; and he must obtain his final discharge from the army. The two crises were almost immediately upon him. On April 19, after only a last fortnight of frantic study, he tried his examinations; and a few days later, at London, he came up before his crucial medical board. The board took its time to reach a decision. For most of one long, agonizing afternoon, the issue was in doubt. But some consideration was providentially given to the fact that he was a student; and eventually after considerable debate, he was placed in category "E", which meant his immediate discharge. "It is hard," he wrote to his mother, "to express adequately my feelings just at this point, but 'glad' is a very poor word." "Glad" was probably also a very poor word for the elation he felt less than a week later when he learnt that he had passed his examinations and was to be awarded his M.A. degree.

When, on the night of April 30, he walked out of Walmer Road Baptist Church after the McMaster University Commencement exercises were over, he realized only too well that for him the hour of decision was at hand. He had won his degree. He had been given his discharge and drawn his pay. He had money in his pocket and funds in the bank. And although the financial assistance given to soldiers of the first World War bore no relation to that enjoyed by veterans of the second, he had enough resources to finance at least the first stage of any further training. What was he to do? Was it to be the church or the law? Or, before he began any professional training at all, would it be wise to push his favourite studies in political economy just a little further? There was prolonged and anxious inward debate; there were discussions, which may have been difficult or even painful, with his friends and the members of his family. All the old arguments in favour of his entrance into the ministry of the Baptist Church were gone over again at length; but the strong disinclination to take this course, which he had felt two years before on the eve of his enlistment, came back now with redoubled force. He knew that he could not become a clergy-man. The ministry of the church of his fathers was not for him.

There remained the law. It was the profession which he had in mind when he first went to McMaster and began to interest himself in public speaking. He was still attracted to it; and he decided that when autumn came he would begin professional legal studies at Osgoode Hall. Autumn, however, was five months away. He had the whole summer before him; and, as always, he was restless and impatient to be busy with something that interested him. He had always wanted to continue his studies in political economy. Why should he not spend the interval before the opening of Osgoode Hall in improving his painfully inadequate knowledge of economics? The University of Chicago, he knew, had a summer school. He decided to go to Chicago for the summer quarter.

V

In Chicago, he was a romantic figure. He had been one of the earliest of the Canadian soldiers to return home, their service completed, seriously wounded, but still whole. Even in Canada, where heavy casualties were an old and sad story, people were apt to break into tears or cheers or congratulations on his appearance in public. In the United States, which had entered the war not much more than a year ago, he drew even more glances and arrested more attention. His tall, slight, awkward, angular figure, bent slightly over his stick and moving forward with painful deliberation, was a romantically conspicuous sight in academic rooms and corridors from which so many young men had departed and to which so few had returned.

He walked about, gradually accustoming himself to student life, noting details, making critical comparisons. Fresh from the reticence and understatement of England and Canada, he was appalled at the "bragging and boasting" which went on in public in Chicago on the fourth of July of 1918. He quickly conceived an antipathy, which was acute at first, against Americans in the mass; but he liked the few individual students and professors whom he came to know at all well in that first difficult and confusing quarter. He took an experimental sample of what the University of Chicago had to offer; but it was a course in economics given by Professor Frank Knight which remained longest and most clearly in his memory. Knight was refreshingly sceptical and provocative in his approach to his subject; and he aroused Innis's interest in economics, not only by giving him a new range of knowledge, but also by making him feel how little he knew. By the time the summer quarter ended, Innis became aware that a curious and yet not entirely unexpected change was taking place in his plans. The summer's work at Chicago had been conceived as a mere refreshing prelude to a much longer period of professional training at Osgoode Hall. But it was not turning out that way at all. His studies in economics were rapidly acquiring a greater and greater prominence in his mind. He was completely absorbed by them. The law seemed to recede into the future. His legal training was indefinitely postponed. He decided to begin work for a Ph.D. degree in economics at Chicago University.

At once, the old problem of his academic career—financial need—returned to hound him. This time his position might have been really serious for, despite his desperate attempts to economize, expenses at Chicago were substantially heavier than he had known before. He had begun to borrow a little from his father; but he was saved from any really grave difficulty by a fortunate turn of circumstance as well as by his own increasingly evident ability. On November 11, the war ended; and the University of Chicago, like every other university on the continent, was now obliged to look forward to an immediate and vast influx of veterans from overseas and civil servants from wartime work in Washington. Every department in every university was suddenly and frantically hunting about for new staff and temporary assistants; and Innis, largely because of his impatient zeal, was already on the spot and had already had time to demonstrate his ability. That autumn he was employed by Professor C. W. Wright, the economic historian, to read and mark papers; and next quarter, the winter quarter of 1919, he took on even more impressive responsibilities. He agreed, under Professor Wright's supervision, to teach an elementary course in economics. His salary, for this part-time assistance, was five hundred dollars a year.

It was an invaluable experience. It gave him useful practice in the kind of work which he now began to suspect he would like to spend his life in doing; and it brought him in contact with an interestingly varied group of students—young boys and girls fresh from the secondary schools, veterans back from the western front, and office workers newly released from wartime employment. One of these latter was a girl named Mary Quayle, who had left her home in Wilmette, near Chicago, for wartime work in Washington and who had just returned to the University to complete the final year of her course. He began to notice her. He found that in her case he could perform the lecturer's duty of fitting a name to a face with surprising ease. Her eyes were wide-set and blue and serious. There was a pensive loveliness in her features and a dignity and elegance in her slight figure. They talked. They went to movies together. She had read a lot, in literary regions where he had not ventured very far. Her intellectual interests were comparable with his, and the quiet determination with which she pursued them equalled his own. By the time spring came he began to realize that he was in love.

It was the spring of 1919. He had now been at the University of Chicago a full year. For three academic quarters he had pursued a steady regime of graduate courses; for three quarters he had marked papers and taught elementary economics for Professor Wright. The systematic instruction of graduate work had been extremely valuable to him. C. W. Wright in economic history, F. H. Knight in economic theory and statistics, J. A. Field on population and standards of living, and J. M. Clark on the economics of overhead costs together provided the guidance and stimulus which were perhaps peculiarly fitted to quicken his interests and capacities. They developed his habitual industry and thoroughness, strengthened his naturally sceptical and philosophic approach to his subjects, and opened new and distant perspectives which tempted him to exploration. The courses had done much for him; but they were not the really creative part of graduate work. The thesis was. It was time for him to set about his thesis in earnest. And he decided to give up teaching for the summer quarter in order to give his entire time to it.

He was moved by a strong inner compulsion, which the war had no doubt strengthened, to take up a theme in Canadian economic development. He asked Professor Wright for a Canadian subject, and Professor Wright suggested that he attempt a history of the Canadian Pacific Railway. All during the summer, with Mary Quayle as his now constant companion, he toiled away at this formidable subject in the Chicago library; and when the summer quarter ended, he paid only the briefest of visits to the farm at Otterville and then set out directly for Ottawa and Montreal in search of original material. On an evening early in September, he sat at a desk in the students' room in the Public Archives of Canada, at Ottawa, writing to Mary Quayle. The room was quiet. The building was almost deserted. He had characteristically secured a pass and was working after the Archives staff had departed; and his desk was encumbered with "musty documents on the C.P.R."

He felt a sudden enormous enthusiasm for his work. He looked forward into the future with confidence and elation. "Just why I should be so happy under such auspices," he wrote in a kind of joyful bewilderment to Mary Quayle, "is more than I can explain." Ottawa, of course, was new to him. He thought Parliament Hill and the view across the Ottawa River to the soft distant line of the Laurentians extraordinarily impressive; and, as he explained gratefully to Mary Quayle, the people at the Archives had gone to all kinds of trouble to dig out important material for him. He was, in fact, the first of a new generation of Canadian historical students, and he was given a generous reception. But there was far more than this in his moment of elation. The whole city, the room in which he sat, with all their associations and suggestions formed an ideal setting for the ambitions which were rapidly taking form and coherence in his mind. In that moment he was gripped by an overwhelming sense of direction and purpose— of destiny. He felt that, with Mary's help, he could do all that he now wanted to accomplish. " . . . Both of us," he told her, "can move mountains."

He came back to Chicago late in September, uplifted by the same feeling of exhilaration and purpose. It was true that the money problem which had been the grey inescapable familiar of his university career, still shadowed him relentlessly. He had given up his teaching job during the summer quarter;

the last of his money had been spent in the visits to Ottawa and Montreal, and in the return to Chicago; and by the middle of October he was definitely hard up. Once again, however, the University came to his rescue with the offer of an assistant-ship in the Department of Political Economy for the autumn quarter of 1919 and the winter and spring quarters of 1920, at the slightly higher salary of six hundred dollars. It was by no means affluence. He had to budget for every copper; and the work in the Department cut into the time that he should have been spending on his thesis and his courses. He had his worries; but he could cope with them in the present and he could see their approaching termination. His eye was fixed upon the future.

The future now stretched far beyond the attainment of his doctor's degree. That was the immediate goal—the goal which he could not fail to reach without a total shipwreck of his plans. He was struggling already with the composition of his thesis and worrying about the rapid approach of his final examinations, written and oral. But he was absolutely deter-mined to complete all the requirements for the degree by the end of the summer quarter of 1920; and although he was at times assailed by nervous apprehensions of the ordeal and painful convictions of his own ignorance, he never really ceased for a moment to assume success. By the end of the summer he would have his degree. He would be free to take a job. And what was it to be? The thought of law had receded into a hazily indefinite future. He wanted to become a pro-fessional economist. And, both because of circumstances as well as because of his own abilities, he had the luxury of choosing among several offers instead of searching desperately for an appointment.

The job he really hoped for and expected to obtain was a

university post in economics. Early in the autumn of 1919, he had received a letter from R. H. Coats, the Dominion Statistician, inviting him to make application for a vacancy in the Internal Trade Division of the Dominion Bureau of Statistics. But this position, which was to be available in December of the same year, was timed too early to be of use to him; and in any case he had no inclination for the Canadian Civil Service. The picture of himself as a teacher and researcher in economics in a university was growing clearer all the time in his mind. He had also reached the firm conclusion that he preferred, if possible, to teach in a Canadian university; and when an offer, at two thousand dollars a year, arrived from Beloit University, a college not far away from Chicago, he decided to turn it down, as he told his mother, "on the chance that a Canadian university will send in an application". He had not long to wait. There was some correspondence with the University of Alberta. There was a firm offer from Brandon College which he decided reluctantly in the end to reject on the ground that the students at Brandon wrote McMaster University examinations and that the Brandon staff did not therefore control its own academic standards. These negotiations ended early in May; and already there was a prospect of a new offer from the University of Toronto.

It came first in the form of an inquiry which reached Innis by the most circuitous of routes. He was immediately interested; this, he told Mary Quayle, "looks very good". "Toronto," he went on to explain to her, "is a very nice place and the literary centre of Canada if not the industrial centre. It is the second largest city. The University has about four thousand students and is with the possible exception of McGill University the best university in Canada, and this by no small margin." During the next few weeks, "the best university in

Canada" made suitable inquiries of Innis's instructors about his ability, but did not follow these up with the expected invitation; and it was not until nearly the end of April that a letter arrived from Professor James Mavor, the Head of the Department of Political Economy at Toronto. Mavor first proposed that Innis should come to Toronto for an interview. Four days later he wrote again informing the anxious candidate that Sir Robert Falconer, the President of the University of Toronto, would be passing through Chicago on May 8 and would see him there instead. May 8 arrived. Innis confronted his future President. Sir Robert was formally polite, but completely non-committal. The suspense continued; but now it was nearly over. On May 11, after he had consulted Professor Mavor, Sir Robert wrote offering a position as "lecturer in economics" at an annual salary of two thousand dollars. And Innis at once accepted.

His immediate future was assured. He had found his opportunity and at the same time accepted an additional compulsion. The attainment of his degree by the end of the summer quarter was now an absolute necessity. He was working, as he so often did, as he perhaps instinctively preferred to do, against time. All possible extra responsibilities had now been shed. The end of his appointment as a teaching assistant might have brought a renewal of his financial difficulties at a most disastrously inappropriate moment; but with the thoughtful kindness which had characterized all their dealings with him, the University authorities now offered him the donship of one of their men's residences, Snell Hall, a post which gave him a free room in exchange for a few administrative duties. He accepted it and there he finished the furious struggle for his degree.

On the last day of July he formally submitted his thesis.

"Chester," he wrote to Mary Quayle, "gasped when I wheeled the trunk load—comprising over six hundred pages—into his office. I was somewhat afraid that he would be obliged to move to other quarters. . . . Until it is accepted or rejected I shall more or less hold my breath." He was holding his breath also for the final written examinations which were to begin the next week and for the oral which was to follow immediately. He was working with feverish intensity, for everything depended upon his effort. The strain was appalling. It seemed endless. And then, suddenly, it was over, and Wright was telling him that he was through. The thesis had been accepted. He had passed all his examinations. He had paid his graduation fees, secured a gown for Convocation, and was walking about unostentatiously with the new brief case which was his fiancée's graduation present. And everybody was congratulating him, on his degree, on his appointment to Toronto, and on his engagement to Mary Quayle.

CHAPTER TWO

I

THE DEPARTMENT OF POLITICAL ECONOMY at the University of Toronto was housed in a tall, three storey red-brick building, built perhaps half a century earlier as a private residence, which stood at 69 St. George Street. It did not provide a great deal of accommodation; but up to that time a great deal of accommodation had not been necessary. Political Economy was at the beginning of a great period of expansion—of which indeed, Innis's own appointment was one obvious manifestation; but at the moment it was still a fairly small Department, with a strength of seven, including the new lecturers and Innis himself. Its head was the tall, thin, bushily bearded Scotsman, James Mavor, who for nearly thirty years had been a prominent, slightly eccentric, and pugnaciously assertive figure in university affairs, and who was now drawing close to his retirement. His interests were wide and extremely varied, his knowledge vast and agreeably unsystematic; and he had done perhaps his most important professional studies in the field of Russian economic history. At that time his principal senior subordinates in the Department were R. M. MacIver, the political scientist, W. Jackman, who was already specializing in transportation, and Gilbert E. Jackson, who taught economic theory, statistics, money and banking. The three juniors were Herbert Marshall, who was soon to leave the Department to take up a post in the

49

Dominion Bureau of Statistics, Hubert R. Kemp, whom Innis had known slightly in the old days at the Woodstock Collegiate, and Innis himself.

For a while he stayed in Hart House, the great, grey stone, collegiate Gothic building, which had been used for military purposes during the war and which was just coming into operation for the first generation of undergraduates. The rooms on its third floor reserved for members of the faculty could hardly have been called luxurious; but they were not sufficiently austere and inexpensive for Innis, and within a few weeks he moved to other quarters on St. Vincent Street, which, for greater economy, he shared with a friend. He was extremely, exhaustingly busy. Like every other young lecturer before and since, he had far too much to do. The autumn was a long, agonizing procession of preparations, lectures, and difficult personal encounters. He had been given three courses to teach—a first year course in the Elements of Commerce for students in the new Commerce Course, a second year course in eighteenth and nineteenth century Economic History and Theory for candidates in honour English and History, and a third year course in Economic Theory for teachers.

Even this, onerous and exacting as it was, was not all. About the middle of October he was approached by representatives of the Workers' Educational Association who begged him to start an evening course in economics in the neighbouring city of Hamilton. It meant, each week, a tiring train journey there and back and a lecture delivered at the fag end of a long day; but he accepted the task with what was almost exhilaration. "All the arrangements have been made about Hamilton . . . ," he wrote to Mary Quayle on November 23. "I am glad it is all settled. It is my first appearance in

Hamilton and also the first appearance of the Workers' Educational Association. I hope I don't let the organization down on its first attempt to branch into other territory than Toronto. . . . We have wonderful opportunities to do things worth while here. It will be of real and genuine service and after all that alone is worth while."

The evening course at Hamilton was not the only innovation of that first year. The launching of the new course in Commerce was a much more important development in the life of the Department; and, for a variety of reasons, Innis had a good deal to do with this enterprise from the start. He had just come from a university which had had considerable experience in providing exactly this kind of training. He believed firmly that it should be based upon a solid foundation of theoretical economics; and he had developed a healthy suspicion of the kind of professional business course which he had learnt in the United States to refer to contemptuously as "bourgeois homiletics". When, fairly early in the autumn, Professor Mavor did his young junior the honour of requesting him to prepare a report on the nature and organization of commerce courses, Innis responded readily. "I am in receipt of your report on the Commerce Course," Mavor wrote to him early in November. "It is exactly what I wanted and is admirably done. I am very glad indeed to have on record the data you have given me. The document will be of the utmost value to us in settling the character of the course for the future. . . . "

The character of the course for the future depended not only upon its programme of studies but also upon the spirit with which they were undertaken. The Commerce Club was founded in the autumn of 1920 with the object of promoting a sense of corporate unity and common endeavour among staff and students. Innis became its first president; and he was the one member of the original executive who continued in office for the second year. "Despite all my protests," he wrote to Mary Quayle, "I am elected president for next year and by acclamation." Many of his students were veterans, much of an age with himself, and scarred by similar experiences; and far from being an aloof and impersonal lecturer, he soon began to make lasting friendships among the members of these first classes. His enormous interest in character and personality was from the first an effective counterbalance to his intellectual austerity and academic detachment. Of all the members of the Department he was perhaps most successful in breathing an air of warm, companionable vitality into the new Commerce Course. And its first generation of students became his conscious and devoted followers.

He was happy in his new job. He was fairly well pleased, though not completely satisfied, with his new academic surroundings. There was—it was extremely obvious—a vast difference between Toronto and Chicago. The superb administrative organization, with its efficiency, accuracy, and comprehensiveness, over which Dean L. C. Marshall had presided at Chicago was noticeably absent at Toronto. In the Political Economy building on St. George Street there appeared to be only one typewriter. There was only one secretary. The filing cabinets were regrettably few. The programme of studies, as set out in the University's Calendar, was a large and somewhat chaotic collection of ill-organized and not too well related courses; and the head of the Department, Professor Mavor, was a man of many acquaintanceships and wide experience, who combined an immense and varied knowledge with an obvious lack of systematic specialization. "It is such a pleasure occasionally," Innis confided to Mary, "to have a real personality in the Department, but there are times when some of L.C.M.'s system might very well be used."

"Both have decided disadvantages," he summed up impartially. Both had decided advantages as well. At Toronto, in some mysterious fashion, there seemed to be a greater interest in people as individual personalities; and even a young and untried lecturer was accorded a respect and a freedom in organizing his work which were decidedly unexpected. It was a tolerant, fairly easy-going atmosphere, which favoured individuals and encouraged individual effort and experimentation; and within fairly short order Innis found time to return to his thesis and opportunity to put in practice some of the techniques he had learnt at the Chicago School of Graduate Studies. He and Hubert Kemp made arrangements for the members of the Commerce Course to visit some typical Toronto commercial and industrial enterprises such as the St. Lawrence market and the Massey-Harris Company; and Innis began to subject his students to a rigorous American regime of regular assignments and frequent tests. Yet here, as soon as he approached Canadian economic history, he encountered difficulties. There was a serious lack of usable materials. The commercially produced maps were deplorably inadequate. And nobody apparently had put together a book of readings or documents.

During the brief Christmas holiday he had returned to Chicago and he and Mary Quayle decided that they would be married early in May just as soon as the winter term was over. "I never dreamed there was so much rehearsing to be done in a wedding," Innis wrote naively in one of the last letters in which he discussed their plans. "I was almost amazed when you told me about having finally timed the wedding march." When he came into the Quayle house that spring evening— a tall, slight figure, walking with a slight limp, and carrying the inevitable stick—he still seemed very much the injured veteran, who had not had time—and perhaps had not permitted himself time—to recover from the scars of the war. Ever since he had reached Otterville in the early spring of 1918, he had been driving himself hard; and even now, apart from a brief honeymoon, there was to be no real period of relaxation. Back in Toronto, where there were still undergraduate examination papers to mark, they succeeded in finding an apartment at 696 Markham Street; and there Innis settled down to a thorough and painstaking revision of his thesis on the Canadian Pacific Railway. He must finish it and finish it soon. Apart altogether from his own desire to see his work in print, the regulations of the Chicago Graduate School required the publication in full of accepted theses. And it was not until the next summer, when Innis's book was already in the press, that the rules were relaxed to permit the substitution of a small printed abstract.

In the autumn of 1921, the departmental changes, of which Innis's own appointment had been the prelude, began to crowd rapidly on each other's heels. Herbert Marshall departed to join the Dominion Bureau of Statistics at Ottawa; and there were two new arrivals from Great Britain. One was Vincent Bladen, a scholar fresh from Balliol College, with whom Innis used to argue on occasion about the merits of an Oxford education; and the other was C. R. Fay, a fellow of Christ's College, Cambridge, who had written to Mavor in the previous autumn, suggesting that he thought of coming to Canada for a few years to study conditions in the Dominion at first hand, and requesting a temporary Canadian appointment. Fay was an established scholar, with something of a reputation, though Innis was ignorant of it when he first heard the name; and his appointment was obviously intended to restore the balance of youth and age in the Department. "Professor Mavor," Innis explained to Mary, "with a smile

that even his bushy beard couldn't hide advanced the argument
that the Department needed some senior professors to steady
the boat until the young crop of junior men reached the age
of discretion." Presumably the need for steadying became all
the greater in the spring of 1922, for then Professor Mavor
himself retired. There was a farewell dinner at the York Club,
and Fay acted as toastmaster. The junior members of the
Department paid something for the dinner and something
also in aid of the publication of Professor Mavor's two-volume
book of reminiscences, *My Windows on the Street of the World*.
And, after this somewhat unusual expenditure, they left with
the rather awed feeling of having made a substantial down-
payment on the purchase of the York Club.

The retirement of Mavor, the appointment of MacIver as
his successor, and the arrival of Fay meant the beginning of a
new and important phase in the life of the Department. During
the next half dozen years its work was broadened and reformed
and its courses of instruction thoroughly reorganized. Innis,
of course, participated in all these discussions and took his
share of the planning; but it was not here that his most important work was being done during these years. He was putting
an immense amount of creative effort into his teaching. He was
going through the arduous and exciting mental labour of
discovering the future field of his research. It was to be the
economic history of Canada, and he was to spend most of his
life in its study. But he was not quite ready to begin yet. And
it was perhaps characteristic of Innis himself—and certainly
symbolic of his work—that he should preface his vast labours
for the discovery of Canada by a brief renewal of his contact
with Europe. On May 27 he and his wife sailed from Montreal
for an extended tour of Great Britain, France, Germany, and
Italy. Among a variety of other letters of introduction, Innis

carried with him a note, which Gilbert Jackson had kindly given to him, to the firm of P. S. King & Son, the publishers, in London. King agreed to publish the *History of the Canadian Pacific Railway*; and just before the return to Canada, after a long summer's hurried travelling, Innis was reading proof and checking references in the National Library in Paris.

II

The publication of *A History of the Canadian Pacific Railway*— it came out during the winter of 1923—marked an obvious period in his career. What was he to do next? He had, of course, no doubt whatever about the main field of his endeavour. When he had first suggested to his supervisor, Professor Wright, that he would prefer a Canadian subject for his thesis, the request was perhaps made instinctively and without too much consideration; but, as time went on and he got to know himself and the ground on which he stood more thoroughly, he began to realize that this impulse had been prompted by some very potent influences. He was conscious of a great and compelling affection for Canada. It was the war, which had taken so many simple Canadian farm boys across the ocean to England and Europe, which had first brought home to him the enormous latent force of this feeling. He was convinced that, through the war, Canada had become a mature country which demanded and deserved the best that her sons could give her. And he had no doubt, as a result of his experiences in England and the United States, that, even for Canada's closest relatives and nearest neighbours, the Dominion was still an unknown and unappreciated country. He felt obscurely that he must work for Canada. Canadians must explain their new nation to the outside world. Above all, Canadians must understand themselves. They must realize whence they had come and where they were probably going.

Innis's role in this process of national self-realization and self-determination seemed obvious. He was an economist with an already established historical bent. His thesis had first taught him the historical method; the course in Canadian economic history, which he had begun to teach in the session of 1921–22, had broadened his knowledge of its possibilities. And—perhaps most important of all—the thesis and the course had combined to show him quite plainly the direction which his next investigations must take. A perfectly gigantic task of travel, research, compilation, and interpretation lay before him. There had been historians—though not very many of them— who had devoted themselves to Canadian politics and constitutional development; but, apart from Adam Shortt, there had been virtually no Canadian economic historians at all. Innis must travel and see the face of the entire half-continent that was Canada; he must ransack its national and provincial archives and libraries for material. He must try to make the subject of Canadian economic history live for his students. New methods, new tools of research, new interpretations were all required. But what was needed above everything else was an original approach to the material, a fresh and revealing point of view.

It was this which Innis now realized that he could supply. A new approach had been revealed to him through the limitations as well as through the breadth of his own previous studies. The *History of the Canadian Pacific Railway* had left him profoundly dissatisfied. He spoke later, in one of the shortest and most famous of his prefaces, of his sense of "the incompleteness of that volume and of all volumes which have centred on that subject and on the subject of Canadian Confederation". These books—his own included—had presented what now seemed to him to be an unhistorical and artificial interpretation of Canadian national development. They had viewed the achievement of Canadian unity, through the creation of Confederation and the building of the Canadian Pacific Railway, as an unnatural achievement, an act of men, done in defiance of geography. Innis was now firmly convinced that this idea was false. He had come to realize, as he worked on his thesis, that the Canadian Pacific Railway had simply recaptured, through the new medium of rail transport, a much older Canadian economic unity which had been based on water communication. Canadians had not, as they kept on insisting with senseless parrot-like iteration, been "fighting geography"; geography had been fighting for them. "The present Dominion," Innis wrote later, "emerged not in spite of geography but because of it."

His task, then, was to return to the original unity. He must get behind the age of Confederation and industrialism, the age of the national policy of protection and the Canadian Pacific Railway, and back to the old communication system and the traffic which it carried. Canada, like every other young country, had been dependent upon the production and sale abroad of a few simple staple products, which could be secured in sufficient quantity and without too much difficulty in the young country, and sold profitably in the metropolitan centres of Great Britain and Western Europe. It was through the sale of staple products that migrants preserved their cultural heritage and supported the burden of civilization in the new world; and the discovery of such commodities was vitally essential to their survival and growth as a colonial people. But in a rigorous north-temperate climate such as that of Canada, the number of available products which could stand the high costs of the long transatlantic voyage in the small ships of the day was inevitably small. Fish had first brought England and France to Newfoundland and the islands of the gulf of St. Lawrence. Furs had taken Frenchmen and Englishmen westward along the interlocked river systems and across the continent to the Pacific coast. Furs had been the basis of the first Canadian transcontinental unity. Innis decided to start with it. He would begin at the beginning of continental expansion. The fur trade would be his subject.

The decision to approach Canadian economic history through the study of trade in staple products or commodities was the most important decision of Innis's scholarly career. Like all great ideas, it was a simple one; but it was adapted, with a strikingly peculiar appropriateness, to the history of Canada. It was his greatest contribution to Canadian studies. And it was, in the main, his own original conception. But he was helped towards its discovery and towards the full realization of its possibilities by the work he had done at Chicago, and in particular by the lectures of Professor C. S. Duncan and the books of Thorstein Veblen. Veblen, whom Innis began to read with great care and attention during his student days at Chicago, was a most important formative influence in his intellectual development. Veblen was concerned with the general effects of machine industry and the industrial revolution in a continental environment; and Innis's design, as he conceived it, was to study the impact of the industrialism of the West European empires upon colonial Canada. Unlike Veblen, Innis was a born historian, with a tremendous irrepressible interest in the facts of experience; but though, in the nature of the case, he could get no historical guidance whatever from Veblen, the Swedish-American scholar did provide him with a general theoretical framework for his ideas. C. S. Duncan, who had lectured on marketing at the University of Chicago, made a more precise and definite contribution. Duncan had stressed the intimate relationship between the physical characteristics of a commodity and the marketing structure built up in relation to it. Innis took over this idea and made it a central feature of his work. *The Fur Trade in Canada*—whose publication lay years ahead—was to open with a brief chapter on "The Beaver". And already he had become absorbed in the development of a system of appropriate techniques which was worked out for the sale of beaver fur.

The great creative decisions had been taken. He had settled upon his general plan of operations as a teacher-scholar for the future. He had made up his mind about his first great piece of research. Obviously he must now round out his knowledge of the existing writings, such as they were, which bore upon any phase of his subject. Obviously he must carry forward with energy his systematic exploration of the Public Archives at Ottawa, and the other public and private archives throughout the country and abroad. He began to collect, for his overworked students, great masses of mimeographed documentary material on the development of the different staple trades. With infinite difficulty, he arranged for the production of new maps which would show the interrelations of the river systems from eastern Canada to the Pacific coast. Books, maps, documents, they were all absolutely essential to him as an historian. Yet they did not by any means constitute the whole of the evidence upon which he hoped to rely. He must see the country, and its economic activities, himself and as soon as possible; and it was obviously sensible to venture into the most remote and difficult areas while he had the strength and endurance of youth. In the summer of 1923, one year after his journey to Europe, he was ready to begin. He and Mary Quayle Innis visited Kingston and

Montreal in order to make a survey of the resources of their libraries on Canadian economic history; and then they travelled west to British Columbia—stopping off at Landonville on their journey—and made the return trip down the coast from Prince Rupert to Vancouver by ship. This, though it was extensive enough, was only a beginning. He determined that next year he would explore the last great surviving region of the fur trade, the Mackenzie River basin. His first son, Donald, was born late in April, 1924. And nearly a month later, when the examination papers were finished and he was finally free, he left for Winnipeg.

III

The year was 1924. It was two years before the first "bush pilots", Oaks, Cheesman and Stevenson, were to begin the north-western commercial air service from Hudson and Sioux Lookout to the new mining area at Red Lake. It was five years before the pilots of the Western Canada Airways were to make their first daring flights down the long valley of the Mackenzie. In the briefest space of time, commercial flying was to revolutionize the entire development of the Canadian north. The work of the prospector, the miner, the trapper, the trader, the missionary, and even the curious traveller, like Innis himself, was suddenly to become infinitely more soft and easy than anybody had ever dreamed it could be. The change was coming—and coming soon. But it had not come yet. It was possible, of course, for Innis and his friend John Long, who was to accompany him on the venture, to make most of the enormous journey down to Aklavik by river steamer. But Innis decided to travel at least the first great stage of their expedition by canoe. In March he was busy making inquiries of the Natural Resources Intelligence Service of the Department of the Interior concerning routes and transport; and late in April he received quotations from Edmonton for an eighteen-foot Hudson's Bay canvas-covered canoe.

"As you see," he wrote to his wife from Peace River on June 10, "we have arrived at our kicking off place. We have our tent put up and at present I am looking out over the Peace River. . . . It looks as though we should have to enjoy it for at least a day more as our canoe has not arrived. It was promised today but the freight doesn't get in until tomorrow. We shall probably get away Thursday morning. Then we have three hundred miles to the next Post Office at Fort Vermilion and I shall drop you a line from there." It was late at night on June 19 before they reached Fort Vermilion. The river was a wide muddy stream, flowing swiftly between steep banks and sown with frequent islands whose flat, white, sandy points, piled with driftwood and swept free of mosquitoes by an unfailing breeze, made ideal camping places. The Peace, Innis wrote later, was "apparently designed for canoeing" though he added cautiously "always, of course, down stream and with a freight canoe." Downstream the swiftly moving river carried them onwards at the rate of about fifty miles a day.

Their route lay down the Peace River to Lake Athabasca, from Lake Athabasca by the Slave River to Great Slave Lake, over the lake into the Mackenzie and then down the "Big River" to Aklavik and the Delta. On June 29, they reached Fort Fitzgerald on the Slave River; on July 6, they camped at Fort Resolution: "I am looking out over Great Slave Lake," he wrote to his wife, "through a maze of tents and teepees. The Indians are all over the place—they are coming in for 'Treaty money'. And of course they all have dogs so that you can imagine what the place is like. We are hoping to go to Hay River as soon as a motor boat comes along." It was two days before they could leave Fort Resolution, for a violent storm of wind and rain beat Great Slave Lake into a fury; but eventually, on the evening of the second day, the small Hudson's Bay tug, *Liard River*, with Captain L. Morten commanding, bore them onwards and across the lake towards the north-west. "The Captain," ran the somewhat intimidating contract which Innis signed on accepting passage in the tug, "has informed me that the *Liard River* is only fitted for the Company's purposes, and is not a passenger vessel in the ordinary sense; consequently the accommodation is only given as an exceptional favour. I, therefore, declare that in taking passage I am willing to accept whatever the vessel may offer in the way of comfort, food, and speed." Innis was glad enough to accept after the hundreds of miles of canoeing down the Peace and Slave Rivers. The *Liard River* gave rough and simple but friendly transport; and in it he settled down to the tortuous journey down the great river to the Arctic.

The long summer, with its wind and sun, its space, and peace, and friendly companionship, had done him an immense amount of good. He had, as it were, shaken off the last of the evil effects of the war. He was starting off on the first great creative period of his scholarly career in an infinitely better physical state than he or his friends would have believed possible only a few years before. The long quiet hours paddling down the Peace, or lying on the sunlit deck of the *Liard River* had given his wounded leg the rest which he himself could not have been compelled to give it in any other circumstances. He never used his stick again. His limp disappeared. He had recovered his health and spirits; and he had come back with a knowledge of the new Canadian northland such as none of his contemporary Canadian scholars would ever possess. The whole vast country of the Peace and Mackenzie Rivers lay spread out before him in a concrete, detailed, vivid and comprehensive panorama. He was intimately acquainted with the workings of the fur trade; he had made friends and acquaintances of dozens of the men who did the hard labour of the north. And he had proved, by a most spectacularly impressive demonstration, that his method of travel and personal inspection could pay very large dividends indeed. He was never again to make such an heroic effort; but the practice of going to the spot and seeing with his own eyes remained throughout a central part of his work.

It was only one part, however. The search for historical documentation was an equally important division of his labour. He wanted to know all kinds of experience—past as well as present. He was, as always, in an eager, impatient hurry to get at the evidence; and the long journey down the Mackenzie, which most men would have considered a more than sufficient effort for one summer, was followed, with only the briefest of pauses, by a voracious attack upon the documents of the fur trade. Early in September, he was back in Ottawa again, working away at his desk in the Public Archives; and the spring term of 1925 had barely finished and the first hot days of early June had only just arrived when he returned to the capital for what was to be a long, unbroken summer of research. The fur trade, of course, was still a main object of this gargantuan labour; but now he had another and more general enterprise on hand. During the autumn he had discussed with Arthur Lower, who was then working in the Public Archives as an assistant to Dr. Adam Shortt, his long-contemplated project of a book of documents on Canadian economic history. And Lower had agreed to collaborate in the work.

It was a hot, energetic, and happy summer. There were, of

course, no Canadian organizations which could help to under-write the cost of such an undertaking and the great American foundations had not as yet given much support to Canadian scholarship. The promoters of the book of Canadian documents had to find their own money and assistance. Hughena, Innis's sister, came down to Ottawa to help in the typing; and Lower was able to secure part of the time of the secretary of the absent Dr. Shortt. The compilers worked away in the manuscript room; and along with them worked others, mainly senior to them in years, of the new generation of Canadian economic and political historians. Arthur Morton from Saskatchewan, Chester Martin from Manitoba, Ross Livingston and Duncan McArthur were all in Ottawa for part of that summer. There were picnics, sails on the lake, fishing trips, and visits with the Lowers and Marshalls; and in August Mary Innis arrived, with Donald, now over a year old, and they rented an apartment for the rest of the summer.

During the next few years, the plan of operations, which Innis had put into such strenuous practice in 1924 and 1925, became an established procedure, which was only slightly varied. Teaching, research, and travelling alternated with each other in a fairly regular succession. During the winter he worked over his courses in economic geography and Canadian economic history and pushed his studies of the fur trade steadily forward. Spring and autumn usually included a few weeks, or a few days, at least, of concentrated research at the Public Archives at Ottawa; and when summer came, he set out on another journey of exploration into one or other of the great Canadian staple trades. In 1926 he struck north to the Yukon to begin his investigation of Canadian mining. In 1927 he visited a long succession of mines, lumber mills and pulp and paper mills in Nova Scotia, New Brunswick, and northern Ontario and Quebec. The early spring of 1928 found him back in such typical northern mining and pulp and paper towns as Cobalt, Haileybury, Rouyn, Kirkland Lake and Iroquois Falls; and on June 1 of that year he sailed for England, at the request of the authorities of the University, to attend the International Geographical Congress at Cambridge, and to carry out systematic investigations of the geography departments of the various universities of Great Britain and Europe.

The academic year which opened in September, 1928, was his ninth. He had gone a long way in the eight years in which he had been a member of the Department of Political Economy at the University of Toronto. He had seized upon a general field of study with extraordinary swiftness and conviction. He had explored it with tireless energy and unremitting perseverance; he had put both the endless drudgery of detailed research and the swift insights of his far-ranging imagination into his work. He had spent his strength, his time, and h s money with an almost reckless abandon. And already the results of his labours had become formidably impressive. His courses in the Department were packed with new material organized in his own original fashion; his yearly list of publications was growing rapidly longer with the passage of every twelvemonth. By 1928, he was doing a good deal of scholarly reviewing, chiefly for the *Canadian Historical Review* and the *American Economic Review*. The *Fur Trade of Canada*, a descriptive analysis of the contemporary Canadian fur trade, had appeared in 1927, in the University of Toronto Studies in History and Economics; and when Innis left Canada for England in June of the following year there were two other enormous manuscripts waiting for publication.

There was almost no financial aid for research in those days;

there was little financial assistance for scholarly publications. And Innis, who had had a quite exceptional piece of good luck in the acceptance of his *Canadian Pacific Railway*, had now to endure the refusals, postponements, and conditional offers which were then the accepted portion of every Canadian academic author. The first draft of the history of the fur trade —a huge, untidy manuscript, with pages cut, corrected, and pasted together again—was completed some time early in 1927. It was first submitted to the University of Toronto Studies Committee and in the end rejected on the ground of its length and the certain great expense of its publication. P. S. King, the firm which had issued the *Canadian Pacific Railway*, was then approached; and King agreed—provided the firm were granted a subsidy in aid of the cost—to publish a small edition of the work. But the University of Toronto was no more prepared to give a small subsidy than it was to undertake the entire risk of publication. The offer of P. S. King & Company had to be declined; and it was not until April of 1928, more than a year after the manuscript had first started upon its travels, that the disappointed and impatient author received his first real encouragement. The Yale University Press—the last firm to which the manuscript had been submitted—replied that it would like to consider publication provided the French passages were translated and the book as a whole slightly reduced. Innis accepted these conditions in principle and eagerly attacked the business of revision. When he left for England in June he was virtually assured that the book into which he had packed a whole new interpretation of Canadian history would at last appear.

The *Select Documents on Canadian Economic History* was a different matter. The material had been transcribed and to some extent arranged, but the work of annotating and editing had not yet been completed. Even so, the manuscript was formidably huge in size. Innis took a sample portion of it over to England with him in the hope of interesting English firms in its publication. He reported to Mary Innis that his luggage was reduced in weight by a pound once he had deposited the sample at the London office of the Oxford University Press; and the secretary of that organization subsequently calculated that if, as Innis said, the submitted portion amounted to only about a third of the manuscript, the whole work would make a book of approximately two thousand pages. In these circumstances, Oxford declined to consider publication, except on a strict commission basis, with the author, or the University of Toronto, paying the entire cost. And the Cambridge University Press, to which the manuscript was then promptly sent, returned an equally discouraging answer. In the end, Innis submitted the manuscript, not to the University of Toronto Studies Committee, which was interested in a different kind of scholarly work, but to the University of Toronto Press, which was then beginning a somewhat more ambitious publishing programme; and the Press decided to undertake the immediate publication of the first great section of the work, from the beginning to 1783, which Innis himself had compiled.

His books, though with some difficulty, were finding publishers. His work was getting to be well and widely known. Three years before he had been made an assistant professor; and his fairly speedy ascent up the academic ladder seemed assured. The Department, which had moved to new quarters in Baldwin House, an old and substantial private residence at the corner of St. George and College Streets, was, in fact, changing rapidly—a state obviously favourable to quick promotion. Patrick Dobbs had come and gone; Alexander

Brady and J. L. McDougall had been appointed lecturers; and A. J. Glazebrook, a senior expert in foreign exchange, had become a special lecturer in banking. But obviously, of course, the most important change came in 1927, when R. M. MacIver, after only five years as head of the Department, resigned to take up a post in Columbia University. A farewell dinner was held; a handsome piece of plate was presented; the usual pleasant speeches were made. And yet—for the succession of the headship was not quite certain—there was something beside pleasantries in a few of the speeches. There were discreet hints and veiled pleas for the future. "It developed," Innis wrote with cheerful cynicism to his wife, "into a most interesting duel—interesting to those who knew."

In the end the University did a perhaps unexpected thing. It appointed E. J. Urwick to the vacant headship. Urwick was a man of sixty, who had only recently resigned after a long career in the University of London and who had had apparently no intention of resuming academic work when he had come out to Canada. He had been prevailed upon, however, to do some lecturing in the Department of Political Economy at Toronto, though, so far, only for one term, the spring term of the academic session 1926-27; and it was with this extremely brief introduction to the personnel and problems of the Department that he became its head at the end of the same academic year. He had been trained in classics at Oxford, had spent ten years as Professor of Social Philosophy at London, and viewed economics and political science with the eye of a philosopher and a humanist. Long before he himself retired from the chair at Toronto, he had come to appreciate Innis's qualities to the full; but at the moment he was only very imperfectly aware of them. He probably regarded Innis as a typical product of the American graduate schools—a dull, plodding, fact-finding scholar with a materialistic outlook on life and a determinist view of the social process. He no doubt saw little promise in him; and in the spring of 1929 he acted upon this first inadequate estimate. He recommended—it was his responsibility as head of the Department—the promotion of a person who was junior to Innis to the rank of an associate professorship. Innis was to remain an assistant professor as before. His colleague would thus be promoted over his head.

Innis's response to this was immediate and emphatic. He was violently angry. It was not that he grudged his colleague his promotion or believed that he had not earned it: he was simply convinced that his own work in the Department was equally deserving of reward. He had, through his researches and travels, begun a fundamental and completely original re-interpretation of Canadian history. His courses, based on new material and with a fresh outlook, had been carefully organized; his string of publications, already fairly lengthy, was rapidly growing. He believed in his own worth and the value of his services; he was convinced that he had been flagrantly underrated and dealt an insupportable injustice. And he acted at once. He did not hint at resigning, or threaten to resign. He resigned. He set about finding another job. "I am writing," he confided to his old friend and adviser, D. A. MacGibbon of Alberta, "to ask whether your Department is in a position to absorb an individual with the qualifications I possess."

The University authorities—it may be fairly confidently assumed—experienced a distinct shock. They had thought that they had to deal with a diffident and docile scholar. They found themselves confronted by an angry and determined man. They decided very quickly that they did not want to lose him and that he must be induced to stay. But there was, as they very well knew, only one way in which he could be appeased. They decided to take it. And Innis, on his part, was being urged by several confidants, including MacGibbon, to moderate his extreme stand and to withdraw his resignation. "I am perhaps less prone than others to take advice," he wrote to MacGibbon, thanking him for his counsel, "but in this case it is most welcome and I think quite sound." He decided to accept the University's offer of an associate professorship and to remain at Toronto; but a bitter after-taste of injury and dissatisfaction remained. "The row is over temporarily," he wrote to his wife, "and I get my promotion to Associate Professor. I am not particularly pleased with it since it was got by sheer brute strength and I don't think a university should be conducted on that basis. . . . I get hot and cold by turns but you must pay no attention to it. However for the time I am vindicated."

IV

The first decade of his career in the University was coming to an end. He was apparently settling down into the normal relationships and activities of his age and profession. He was a householder, a father, a family man. He had built a house on Chudleigh Avenue, in the rapidly growing north of Toronto. His elder daughter, Mary Ellan—it was the Manx spelling of the name—was born in 1927; his second son Hugh three years later, in 1930; and his younger daughter, Anne, in 1933. He had the properties and responsibilities of the average citizen; but, in many ways, nobody could have been more oddly unusual. He often seemed to take little interest in his physical surroundings. Gardening, home improvements, family enterprises—the normal avocations of the academic suburbanite—

did not afford him long hours of pleasureable relaxation. He was often completely oblivious of what in North America are regarded as the ordinary duties of parenthood. Yet, in his own different and special way, he was an excellent father and a devoted family man. His driving inexhaustible urge for the experience which only travel could bring took him frequently and for long periods away from Toronto; and, even when he was at home, his concentration upon his books and papers was so close and exclusive, that sometimes he scarcely seemed aware of the children's presence in the house. He did not do a great many things with them. He had never learnt to play games. Charlie Chaplin and the Marx Brothers were the only movies to which he went with real delight. And he invariably left the purchase of all the children's Christmas and birthday presents to his wife. Yet, though he was often absent from home, he was always, almost as soon as he had started upon a journey, unhappily eager to return. He did not give as much time to his children as many fathers; but the time he did give was given completely. He never condescended to them. He never talked down to them. They had his serious and exclusive attention.

He had come of sober, hard-working, and strongly religious stock; but he was moulding the basic materials of his character with all the individual freedom which was perhaps the greatest gift of his inheritance. Organized religion, which had played such an important part in the formative years of his boyhood and early youth, had ceased to have any significant meaning for him; and he became a gentle, unassertive, but convinced agnostic. His belief in the laborious accumulation of facts was balanced by the swift flights of his far-ranging imagination. The austerity of his devotion to the abstractions of scholarship was qualified by his irrepressible human interest in people.

He had scores of friends and acquaintances now in all parts of Canada and in all walks of life. He viewed them and their affairs in an increasingly tolerant, easy-going, quizzically humorous fashion. He had a quick eye and ear for traits of character, tricks of speech, revealing phrases or gestures; and his appetite for good stories was rapidly getting to be enormous. He liked people who shared his own amusement in the unending comedy of human affairs; and he was beginning now to find more time for the lazy exchange of impressions, anecdotes, absurdities, and banter.

The new decade—the decade of the 1930's—brought with it a variety of important changes in his life and work. It meant, in the first place, an obvious change in the subject matter of hi. principal research. The years 1929 and 1930 were spent in putting the final touches to the big projects of the 1920's. During the winter of 1929, the proofs of *Peter Pond* were being corrected; the revised manuscript of the *History of the Fur Trade in Canada* was dispatched to the Yale University Press early in May; and at intervals through the summer months an avalanche of galleys for the *Select Documents in Canadian Economic History* kept descending upon him. "My plans are still unsettled," he wrote to MacGibbon in June, "but I want to see Hudson Bay some time this summer to round out my knowledge of the north country—perhaps I should say to complete my introduction to the north country." The "introduction", as he called it with characteristic modesty, had grown through an intimate acquaintanceship into a profound knowledge. He meant to be thorough; but he had no time to lose. The days of his heroic wanderings in the north-west were over. And the journey that summer through the new mining country up to Churchill was the last of them. In 1930, the *Fur Trade in Canada* was published. He had given almost a decade to it. And the work of the 1920's was done and ended.

Already he had turned to another and a perhaps still more formidable project. He had, he believed, demonstrated the validity of the approach to Canadian economic history through its successive staple products. He was anxious to apply the method to other industries in other regions and ages; and he turned from the continental fur trade to the fisheries of the North Atlantic. It was a highly significant moment in his life as a scholar when one June day in 1930 he set out eastward for Newfoundland and Labrador. "The city is very much as one expects—" he wrote to his wife from St. John's, Newfoundland, "more or less ranged round a bowl at the bottom of which is the harbour. Mountains of rock all over the place— walking up and down these through the afternoon left me almost done in. . . . I came . . . through a fishing village—all sorts of little shacks perched on the side with fish staging all over the place and small boats out in front. . . . I walked around the end of the harbour and along the outer side to the light- house at the entrance—more fishing villages with their goats, chickens, fish nets, and so on. One breathes, eats, sees, and talks nothing but cod. . . . The place has been an absolute gold mine and coming here is much the best thing I could have done from the standpoint of finding out about the industry." He was "finding out about the industry" with his usual tireless energy and incredible speed. In 1930, his first essay on the fisheries, "The Rise and Fall of the Spanish Fishery in New- foundland", was presented to the Royal Society—since Innis himself was not yet a fellow of that august body—by Chester Martin of Winnipeg; and in 1931, this was followed by a paper read at the annual meeting of the Canadian Historical Association, and entitled, in Innis's best sweeping style, "An Introduction to the Economic History of the Maritimes

74

(including Newfoundland and New England)". Three weeks after the paper was read he was away again for another month's "field work" in Gaspé and the Canadian Labrador.

The change of theme was important, for his own personal studies were the heart of Innis's life as a scholar; but it was not the only, nor perhaps the most important, change which was ushered in in the early 1930's. To a very large extent, Innis had spent the previous decade in working out his own approach to Canadian economic history and in proving its validity and value. In the main, his work had been done in his own lectures, his own researches, his own travels to the far corners of Canada. It had been lonely labour, for in those early days he was a virtually unaccompanied adventurer. But, for a variety of reasons, he was never to be so solitary again. He had triumphantly proved his point. His success was making him well known and much sought after. And yet this was not the only explanation of the sudden prominence which his ideas seem to gain in the early 1930's. His own status had unquestionably improved; but so also had the position of political economy, the subject for which he stood. It was obviously— and in his view dangerously—growing more and more important in the university, in government, in the nation as a whole.

The best illustration was the nearest to home. The rising influence and prestige of the Department of Political Economy in the University of Toronto was manifest. The Department had moved again, for Baldwin House could no longer accommodate both History and Political Economy; and it was now established at 273 Bloor Street West in the old and rambling building, so well known to Innis, which had once housed McMaster University. The old honour course in Commerce and Finance had been dropped some time before; the new

Bachelor of Commerce course, now under the supervision of Gilbert Jackson, and the honour course in Political Science and Economics had both been reorganized. It was quite apparent that these two courses were taking an increasing proportion of the best students in the university, at the expense of older and better-staffed disciplines; and inevitably, as the decade of the 1920's had drawn to a close, the Department began to expand in numbers. C. R. Fay, who had come to Canada for a visit of five years and who actually stayed ten, finally left in 1931 to return to Cambridge. No person of comparable experience was appointed to succeed him; but the arrival of C. A. Ashley, L. T. Morgan, J. F. Parkinson, and Irene Biss meant a great and fairly swift increase in the numbers of assistant professors and lecturers. These juniors were soon followed by D. C. MacGregor and A. F. W. Plumptre, the first of a number of Innis's own students to be appointed to the staff in Political Economy. And Innis, who had joined the Department just over a decade before, suddenly found himself a member of its senior directorate.

He was conscious of his new position and quite prepared to exert his new influence. He took a more active part in the Department's highest counsels. He had more to do with the policy of the University as a whole. The mission which had taken him to the International Geographical Congress in England in 1928 was now continued in a search for a scholar, at the level of an associate professor, who would begin formal instruction in the University in geography. He took all these matters fairly easily in his stride. He obviously enjoyed the making and implementation of policy. And normally his relations with his colleagues were excellent. He was courteous, tolerant, fairly easy-going. He was ready for compromises and agreement. But, at the same time, where a principle seemed to be involved, he could be stubborn in opposition and extremely tenacious of his own point of view. And poor Urwick, the urbane and kindly humanist who had been called upon to preside over the deliberations of a group of very able and determined men, was sometimes driven almost to despair. "The administration of the Department cannot go on if disagreements are carried beyond a certain point," he once rebuked Innis, "and frankly I think that you have carried yours too far."

The work of the Department, with its increasing burdens, and complexities, and occasional rows, was one aspect of the widening sphere of Innis's activities. Another, equally important, was the growing sense of corporate unity, and the increasing measure of co-operation, among the economists and political scientists of Canada as a whole. Innis, in his early days at Toronto, had been a solitary student of Canadian economic history; and his loneliness had been deepened by the comparative isolation of the social scientists at Toronto from their fellows in the other universities of Canada. A state of detachment, of unawareness of each other's scholarly progress, had been largely characteristic of the members of Canadian universities in the past. It was to be so no longer. Innis himself, through his work in the archives in Ottawa and his travels through Canada—he never passed through a university town without visiting its principal scholars in history and economics —had done much to break down this isolation. And now he and others set to work to create institutions through which this new-found sense of comradeship could be expressed. In 1929, the Canadian Political Science Association—which had collapsed some years before after only a single meeting— was effectively reorganized; and the sessions which were held in Ottawa, late in May, 1931, at which Innis read his paper

"Transportation as a Factor in Canadian Economic History" constituted one of the first great meetings of the revived association.

National societies were one expression of the new sense of identity and the new readiness for association. But there were other important ventures in co-operation which were begun by the economists, historians, and political scientists of Canada during the early 1930's. Of these perhaps the most significant was the large-scale co-operative series, planned to include a substantial number of volumes by different hands, and devoted to some major aspect of the country's development. There had, of course, been earlier series—the biographical series, *The Makers of Canada*, and that vast Domesday inquiry, *Canada and its Provinces;* but already these efforts belonged to a dead past. Between them and the new enterprises there lay the dividing tragedy of the War of 1914-18. Innis and the other young or youngish men of the 1930's had new points of view and new evidence. They had something of their own that they wanted to say. They were becoming increasingly aware of their co-operative resources; and at the same time— probably as a natural consequence of the evidently growing strength of Canadian scholarship in history and the social sciences—the great American foundations, for what was really the first time, began to give substantial financial support to Canadian research and writing. The results were two large-scales series of volumes, planned and largely written by Canadians. The first was *Canadian Frontiers of Settlement*, edited by W. A. Mackintosh, Innis's friend at Queen's University, Kingston, and W. L. G. Joerg; the second was an even larger series, sponsored by the Carnegie Endowment for International Peace and edited by James T. Shotwell, under the general title *The Relations of Canada and the United States.*

Innis, as might have been expected, gave aid to both these projects. His advice was not infrequently requested in the planning of the *Canadian Frontiers of Settlement*; and in 1936 he contributed to it the short monograph, *Settlement and the Mining Frontier*, which formed half of the ninth and last volume in the series. But unquestionably he gave much more of his time and effort to the other, even larger co-operative scheme, the *Relations of Canada and the United States*. He was present at the first conference, called at Shotwell's request in the summer of 1932, which settled the general plan of the series. "The New York trip was rushed—" he reported characteristically to Mary Innis, "went down Thursday night and got back Saturday morning. . . . We covered so much ground I was dizzy . . . but we did try to get things under way. I tremble at the amount of work involved. . . . "

He was made editor of the studies written by Canadians on the economic aspect of Canadian-American relations; and in the end wrote important prefaces for four of the volumes. As editor, he was tolerant, easy-going, even a little nonchalantly impatient, as was his wont, of routine problems of editorial detail. But upon two points of principle he took a very firm stand indeed. He did not propose to "buy" Canadian scholarship or to surrender its autonomy. Canadian research was not to be diverted away from its natural channels of development by the persuasive inducements of the new series; and Canadians must have full responsibility for their own contributions to the joint project. Innis declined to accept any direction or supervision from the United States, except that of the general editor; he insisted on the independence of Canadian scholarship. "So important do I regard this principle," he wrote in a draft letter defining his position, "and with such difficulty has it been conceded in the case of similar projects directed from Great Britain and from the United States that I feel that it will be necessary to withdraw from further co-operation with the work, unless it is given full weight. . . . I cannot afford, for the sake of my position in the University and in the project, to be charged with conceding a principle which has been gained at considerable cost."

This was plain speaking; but it was not untypical of the time. It reflected Innis's awareness of his own maturity and of the resources which lay behind him. For the first time since the war it had become possible for Canadian social scientists, through co-operative effort, to accept the responsibility of a great scholarly undertaking. Their sense of corporate unity was growing. They were conscious of their increasing influence and prestige in the universities. And they were also aware— gladly in some cases but very apprehensively in others—of the rapidly growing importance which they were acquiring in the eyes of government and society. This had not been true—not, at least, so generally true—in the past; but it was to remain a prominent feature of the 1930's. The first three decades of "Canada's century", the three decades during which prosperity had been so constant that Canadians had almost come to believe it was theirs by divine right, had ended in economic collapse and political danger. The decade of the 1930's began with the greatest depression of modern times. It closed with the greatest war of modern times. And, as the few brief years between these two catastrophes sped swiftly away, the Canadians, like the other unhappy, bewildered, and frightened peoples of West European–American civilization, began to call their leaders to account and to question every policy, party, and principle of their national life.

Inevitably the scholars were drawn into this anxious inquiry. They began to take part in this agitated debate. They were moved to do so partly by their own scholarly interests and their very great natural concern in national affairs; but they were influenced also by the evident popular assumption that they had something to contribute and by definite governmental requests that contributions should be made. There was lots to do. Everybody had his own little specialty. The historians and political scientists took up the questions of the Canadian federal constitution and Canadian relations with the outside world. The economists devoted themselves to the great general problem of the origins, incidence, and cure of the depression. Foreign policy, the right to neutrality in war, Dominion-provincial relations, constitutional amendment, commercial policy, social welfare, public finance—they were all, in all their endless ramifications, discussed, debated, and argued with passionate enthusiasm and conviction. The scholars wrote articles. They wrote monographs. They collaborated in large co-operative survey volumes. But they did much more than this. Books and articles were, after all, their traditional business; but now, at a dozen open and inviting points, they began bursting into the realm of public affairs.

They became royal commissioners or the research assistants of royal commissions. They sat on public boards and took part in official surveys and investigations. They appeared as expert witnesses before parliamentary committees. All this advice and assistance was offered with the idea of supplying guidance for remedial action inside the existing economic, social, and political framework of the country. The suggestions went far; but in the eyes of some discontented members of the academic fraternity, they did not go nearly far enough. These people wanted much more positive and drastic action. They were, in fact, the "hot gospellers", the economic and social evangelists, who insisted, like all evangelists before and since, that society must be "born again", and that the prelude to the new birth could only be the destruction of the old "system" of capitalistic sin and corruption. They preached with fervour. They also practised. All doubt about their political allegiance was quickly ended. They became prominent members of the League for Social Reconstruction, which was the intellectual avant-garde of the new socialist movement in Canada. They were regarded—and with becoming modesty regarded themselves—as the "brains trust" of the C.C.F. party.

V

Innis was not in the slightest degree impressed by the new prestige which the scholar had acquired; and he was under no illusions about its origins. "The question as to the place of the economist has not arisen prior to this depression," he told the members of the Liberal-Conservative Summer School in Newmarket in September, 1933, "chiefly because no other depression has been so serious and because other depressions have been solved successfully by the politicians." It was a new position in which the social scientist found himself—new and dangerous, both for himself and the state. The social scientist was sensitively conscious of his responsibilities to a defeated and prostrate society. All too frequently, in his natural desire to relieve human misery, he was led on to shrill extremes of confidence or emphasis. "He has assumed that he could compete with demagogues and his assumption has proven to be palpably wrong, except to those economists who have become demagogues themselves in the competitive process." In the competitive process, economists, particularly "messianic" economists, had been perfectly prepared to claim infallible wisdom and to propose incontrovertible solutions. "But let me warn you," Innis declared with blunt directness, "that any exposition by any economist which explains the problems and their solutions with perfect clarity is certainly wrong."

"I am sufficiently humble," he went on, "in the face of the extreme complexity of my subject to know, first, that I am not competent to understand the problems much less to propose solutions. . . . " He had no belief at all in the wisdom of any sweeping, general cure-all. He distrusted the efficacy of particular remedies, reached in isolation, for particular problems. He pleaded, instead, for the rapid but very careful reform of existing policies and the creation of new and more delicate machinery with an eye always to their intricate interrelations in the national economy as a whole. There had always been, he reminded his listeners, economic planning in Canada; but a vast extension of economic planning was now obviously necessary. "I have indicated the inevitability of planning in Canada," he concluded, "—it remains for the economist, realizing his limitations, to render the best advice of which he is capable that the plans may not do more harm than good to the economic structure. . . . Economists cannot compete with politicians. The specialized character of the subject makes public discussion prohibitive. While the economist is forced to assume an increasingly smaller role in public discussion, the demands for his services in the state become increasingly great. . . . He can only concentrate on the causes of disturbance and prepare himself for the occasion in which the politician may dare to consult him."

This was an accurate description of his own activities during the early years of the depression. Yet he was not simply "concentrating on the causes" of the existing disturbance. He was, as always, persistently carrying on his fundamental researches in Canadian economic history. He found time, in the early summer of both 1931 and 1932, for some more "field work" for his fisheries studies in the Maritime Provinces, Labrador, and the Magdalen Islands. In 1933, when he went to England as a delegate to the Sixth Annual Conference for the Scientific Study of International Relations, he did not forget his research; and in between luncheons, dinners, sessions, discussions, visits to co-operatives and hurried travel in England and France, he managed to put in a good deal of time in the Cambridge Library, the British Museum, and the Public Record Office. Nothing must be permitted to interrupt seriously the prosecution of his work on the fisheries, the second great staple in British North American history. He gave it time—a great deal of time every year. But it did not receive all his attention. In his view, it was an obvious obligation of the economist to try to understand the nature and origins of the current depression. He was "concentrating on the causes" of the existing disturbance. He was even "preparing himself for the occasion" on which a politician might consult him.

His method, as always, was a combination of field work and documentary study. In the late summer of both 1932 and 1933 he made brief visits to the West in order to see for himself something of the devastation which the depression had wrought in the Prairie Provinces; and at all times he was working hard to master the new evidence and to fit it into his knowledge of the main trends of Canadian economic development. The incidence and alleviation of the depression was a subject which crept irrepressibly into the preface of *Problems of Staple Production in Canada*; it was the main theme of *The Canadian Economy and its Problems*, which he edited with A. F. W. Plumptre and for which he wrote the general introduction. These books, like the article which he contributed to the *Economic Journal* on "Economic Conditions in Canada in 1931–32", were designed in the main for a specialist academic audience. But such work was receiving wider publicity than it had ever done before; and in other, more obvious ways, he was accepting, and perhaps seeking, a closer relationship with business men and politicians. In the summer of 1932, he agreed to write an article on the depression for the *Financial Post*. He appeared at the Liberal-Conservative Summer School held at Newmarket in September, 1933, and read a satirically realistic paper, heavily weighted with closely argued "appendices". In the autumn of 1932 he was in communication with the Prime Minister, R. B. Bennett, over certain phases of governmental policy in the depression.

It was not, however, until the spring of 1934 that he received an invitation to make a direct and important contribution to public affairs. On May 25 a confidential telegram arrived unexpectedly from Angus L. Macdonald, the Premier of Nova Scotia. "Would you be available this summer," the telegram read, "for post on economic commission to be set up by Province of Nova Scotia. Difficult to say when commission will sit due to arrangements with English chairman, but hopeful can get Englishman latter part of July or early August. Please wire collect if your arrangements for the summer permit acceptance." There was no doubt in Innis's mind about the reply which the prepaid telegram would carry. He would accept. He was pleased with the invitation. He knew that he deserved it. He had, indeed, "prepared himself for the occasion" in which a politician might dare to consult him; and his preparation had been made in the only way which he considered legitimate. He had not written articles attacking the Bennett government, or extolling the programme of the Liberals, or proving the dreadful effects of federal policies on the economy of Nova Scotia. He had simply studied the history and economy of Nova Scotia. He had visited the province repeatedly. He had made a sustained effort, lasting now for nearly five years, to understand the historical development of its oldest industry.

Another scholar, less thoroughly acquainted with the problems which loomed ahead of him, would probably have spent the early summer in anxious preparation. Still another scholar, wiser if not more learned, would doubtless have fortified himself for the approaching ordeal by taking a long peaceful holiday. But Innis did neither. For the greater part of July he worked steadily away at fisheries documents in the Public Archives and Parliamentary Library in Ottawa; and early in August, when he got off the train at Halifax, the Premier was on the platform to meet him, and his fellow-Commissioners, Professor J. H. Jones and Dr. Alexander J. Johnston, had already arrived. Jones, the "English chairman" to whom Macdonald's telegram had referred, was Professor of Economics and Head of the Department of Commerce in Leeds University. He arrived, naturally, with very little knowledge of Canada as a whole and still less of Nova Scotia; but Innis reported in an early letter to his wife that he was "a very able and likeable fellow". The most richly satisfying companion, from Innis's point of view, was, however, the third Commissioner, Alex Johnston.

Johnston was a veteran politician and civil servant, now settling down into the comfortable old age of retirement, who had been a member of the Nova Scotia assembly, a member of Parliament, and, for over twenty years, Deputy Minister of Marine and Fisheries. He had almost all the qualities which, in a public man, were likely to interest and impress Innis. A long and varied range of experience, an enormous memory for personalities and events, a great capacity for telling stories in a style rich with phrases of his own invention, and a wise, tolerant, humorous attitude to life in general—they were all his. He was the kind of politician whose company Innis instinctively relished, just as he instinctively grew restive in the presence of a scholar who had suddenly entered public life. The scholar turned politician through messianic impulses was, in his view, only too apt to be a narrow, arrogant, fanatical, and dangerous man. But Johnston, passing through all the usual stages of his trade as apprentice and journeyman, had grown old and wise in the craft and mystery of politics. Innis delighted in him. He kept on expatiating about him to his wife. He is "a delightful man—" he wrote, "always full of tales and fun—talking about teetotal hell and so on. It has been worth it to meet him."

They stayed some time in Halifax to receive submissions, hear evidence, and digest the formidable brief on behalf of the Province which had been submitted to them by Norman McL. Rogers. And then they set out on their brief, rapid perambulation of Nova Scotia. "We meet the mayors, M.Ps., and various officials," Innis explained to Mary Innis, "and hear all the evidence we can on a great variety of subjects. Of course we put in all sorts of questions and by the end of the day are exhausted. Fortunately I get to bed in semi-reasonable time . . . and I am able to stand the strain without too much loss of energy. . . . Johnston's son drives the car—a very good but fast driver, and we cover as much ground as possible. . . . The rest of the retinue includes a secretary, a stenographer, and a press correspondent. We travel in two cars—not pretentious cars but such as eventually reach their destinations. . . . I shall be glad when the travelling is over and when we start to get at the report." This was a wish he repeated several times as the Commission cars sped on their hurried journey to the south-west and then back to the north-east of the peninsula. Actually the tour, long as it seemed, took less than three weeks. By September 9 they were back in Halifax.

Then came the report. By their terms of reference, the Commissioners were required to investigate and consider "the effect of the fiscal and trade policies of the Dominion of Canada upon the economic life of the Province of Nova Scotia", "the adequacy of present financial arrangements between the Dominion of Canada and the Province of Nova Scotia", and "any other matter affecting the economic welfare of Nova Scotia, or its relation to the Dominion of Canada." It was a tall order to fill after such a hurried investigation; and, late in September, while Jones went on to Montreal and Ottawa, Innis was already busy arranging his own ideas and making preliminary drafts. "I have been writing furiously all week," he wrote to his wife, "and have the back of the thing broken and should have it pretty well covered by the time Jones gets back. We then go into a 'huddle', as Johnston would say, and decide on general principles, and it may be we will go on to Toronto so that I can be on hand at the first of the week."

In the end they went on to Toronto in order that Innis might be present for the opening of the autumn term at the University. And at Toronto the "huddle" seriously commenced. At once a slight but significant difference of approach and emphasis disclosed itself among the Commissioners. Jones, with the concurrence of Johnston, preferred to give the federal Canadian tariff a place of central prominence, and to bring out its nature and injurious consequences by a comparison between it and a free trade system. Innis was prepared to go quite a distance in acknowledging the burdens which the Canadian tariff had placed upon Nova Scotia; but he evidently could not help feeling that the Jones comparative method was too narrow and theoretical. His own inclination, as always, was towards a more historical treatment. His own preference was for an "emphasis on the national policy in the broad sense rather than in the narrow fiscal sense". Yet, with some important exceptions, his conclusions and recommendatations did not differ seriously from those of his colleagues. He did not wish to write a formal "minority" report; but on the other hand he was an individualist who was not prepared on this occasion to surrender his identity. In the end he hit upon the idea— which was probably fairly satisfactory to all concerned—of writing a separate, but "complementary" report.

VI

The *Report of the Royal Commission, Provincial Economic Inquiry* came out early in December, 1934. The remainder of the month was taken up by a brief but highly necessary recuperation and by watching, with mingled annoyance and satisfaction, the press reviews of the *Report*. It had been a strenuous—an even |unusually strenuous—year. There was not to be quite so much prolonged and grinding labour in 1935; but, at the same time, 1935 was to have, in various important ways, its own special significance. It brought Innis further recognition and new honours; it was marked by some trenchant declarations of his principles; and it saw the first promising fruits of plans which had been carefully worked out during the preceding years.

He had been made a fellow of the Royal Society of Canada in 1934. It was becoming more and more probable that he would be Urwick's successor as head of the Department of Political Economy. The projects over which he had toiled in the early 1930's were getting close to, or had reached, the production stage. The correspondence with Shotwell and

J. B. Brebner of Columbia University concerning the new series, *The Relations of Canada and the United States*, increased in volume. Arrangements were finally made with the Yale Press in the United States and the Ryerson Press in Canada for the publication of the projected volumes; and Shotwell proposed, as a public introduction to the series and an experiment in "adult education" in North American good neighbourhood, to call a conference on Canadian-American relations at the St. Lawrence University, New York State, in June. The first studies in this big publishing venture would soon be out now; and, in the meantime, another, purely Canadian enterprise in scholarly publication, to which Innis had given a great deal of his time and consideration, at last got under way. For years the *Canadian Historical Review* had been the one learned journal in the general field of Innis's interests; but now, in February, 1935, the *Canadian Journal of Economics and Political Science* made its appearance. And in April, at the Old Mill Restaurant in Toronto a dinner was given in celebration of the event and in honour of the *Journal's* managing editor, Vincent Bladen, and Innis.

The appearance of the *Journal* was important for Innis for another and special reason. The contents of the first issue impelled him to begin a reassessment and definition of his views respecting the meaning and value of the social sciences. In the first number of the new publication, E. J. Urwick had contributed an essay, "The Role of Intelligence in the Social Process", in which he had taken up, very emphatically, an extreme relativist position. He had denied the possibility of objectivity in the observer when confronted with living reality; he had refuted the claims of the social sciences to be regarded as real sciences in any valid sense of the term. These conclusions, expressed with all of Urwick's adroit persuasiveness and provocative wit, were too much for Innis. Nobody was more fully convinced than he of the limitations and weaknesses of the social sciences. He knew that, even inside the universities, social scientists were far from immune to the "numerous and subtle" dangers of bias; and he was convinced that these dangers were multiplied as soon as social scientists became at all seriously involved in activities outside the university, at the request of business, church, or state, or even in the service of what was believed to be the "public interest". As was his habit, he filled in Urwick's philosophic generalizations with a long, dismaying list of concrete particulars; but even this portentous enumeration of biases did not, in the end, shake his basic confidence and faith. He could not bring himself to accept Urwick's sweeping conclusions. "The innumerable difficulties of the social scientist," he wrote in his reply to Urwick's argument, "are paradoxically his only salvation. Since the social scientist cannot be 'scientific' or 'objective' because of the contradiction in terms, he can learn of his numerous limitations. The 'sediment of experience' provides the basis for scientific investigation. The never-ending shell of life suggested in the persistent character of bias provides possibilities of intensive study of the limitations of life and its probable direction. . . . The habits or biases of individuals which permit prediction are reinforced in the cumulative bias of institutions and constitute the chief interest of the social scientist."

Innis had attempted a considered reply to Urwick's argument, for Urwick's argument was a serious attack upon his position. There was no further discussion of the subject in the *Journal*; but the debate did not, in fact, end here. A few months later Innis was faced with what was in essence a political version of Urwick's case. At the annual meeting of the Canadian

Political Science Association, held at Kingston in May, 1935, F. H. Underhill read a paper on "The Conception of a National Interest". Underhill had declared his own political allegiance by becoming a prominent member of the League for Social Reconstruction; and he now denounced his fellow historians and social scientists for their failure to make a similarly full and public profession of their faith. They must, he informed them, admit that the root conflict of interest within the national society was a class conflict. They must acknowledge that the existing crisis was a crisis of capitalism. They must risk their "academic integrity" by making up their minds as to what Canadian "social objectives" ought to be, and fearlessly publishing their findings. In effect, it was Urwick's argument, much simplified and carried to a practical conclusion. Urwick had sought to prove the theoretical difficulty, if not impossibility, of pursuing the scientific investigation of the social process; Underhill contended that the pretence of scientific detachment ought to be abandoned and a definite stand taken for social righteousness' sake.

Innis was not prepared to accept either one of these positions; but he considered the second more objectionable than the first. Urwick's argument was a solid philosophical argument; Underhill's seemed to be an ordinary party case. The naively complacent claims of a new party to be "above party", to be "not just another party", left Innis unimpressed and vaguely uneasy. It was entertaining to see sensible people apparently assuming that J. S. Woodsworth, rather than R. B. Bennett or W. L. M. King, was the incarnation of God's providence for the Dominion of Canada; but the effects which their missionary zeal was likely to have on universities in general and the social sciences in particular aroused in him a definite apprehension. "The weakness of the social sciences in Canada," he wrote to one correspondent, "and the aggressiveness of a new party looking about for any substance which it may devour involve the breaking down of our intellectual position. Whatever may be said about the old parties, there has never been the flagrant attempt to prostitute intellectual interest which has characterized the recent arrival. . . . I cannot conceive how anyone can have solved the problem of the Canadian economy and become so convinced of his solution as to start preaching and to berate those of us who are trying to do a decent job in our own way. There is much to be said for the Marxian approach to Canadian history, but not sufficient to support absolute certainty. Intellectual honesty and curiosity demand fresh interpretations and not the same interpretation. . . . The country is full of so-called leaders always anxious to seize upon anything which has the ring of truth in it and a thoroughly sound and scholarly piece of work will be taken up by all parties and make far more advance than years of preaching. We suffer from a plethora of preachers and a scarcity of intellectual effort. . . . But I am becoming weary of preaching against preaching. . . . "

He was not done with the "hot gospellers" yet. The position of the social sciences in an age of over-confident popular dogmatism on economic and social matters continued to interest and worry him during the summer of 1935. Late in June, taking his son Donald with him, he went west to the Pacific coast to teach Canadian history in the University of British Columbia Summer School. It was an uneventful, relatively easy summer, in sharply pleasant contrast with the fatigues of the previous August; and although he found the daily two-hours' lecture something of a burden, his health noticeably improved and his progress with the giant study on the fisheries became much more satisfactory. Yet, in the midst of this productive tranquillity, the defence of Canadian scholarship against the clamour of the depression continued to trouble him. When it became his turn, as an instructor in the Summer School, to deliver a popular public lecture, he chose the subject "Discussion in the Social Sciences"; and after his return to Toronto, the federal general election of that autumn and a spate of tracts for the desperate economic times kept the subject vividly fresh in his mind. In a review, called "For the People", in the *University of Toronto Quarterly*, he dismissed *Social Planning for Canada*, by the Research Committee of the League for Social Reconstruction, in a brief, satirically contemptuous notice. He had become exasperated by what he called "the tyranny of talk", "the travelling comedians who masquerade as economists and prophets" and "the post-war adventurers in universities" who turn "to political activity and popular acclaim during depressions". "Discussion," he declared roundly, "has become a menace rather than a solvent to the problems of a complex society." It was a highly unpopular position; and Innis, through the very vehemence of his dissent, became a somewhat detached and lonely figure. Even a few of his friends regarded his statements with the lifted eyebrows of disapproval. He was gravely reprimanded, on one occasion, for his failure to recognize his "communal obligations". He was solemnly warned of the insidious fascist implications of his deplorable attack on freedom of discussion.

In the meantime, however, his position in the University, which was what he cared about most, grew steadily stronger; and in July, 1936, he was appointed Professor of Political Economy. It was the prelude to another year of strenuous work. In retrospect the quiet summer at British Columbia seemed like a brief, placid interlude in the uninterrupted grind of his labour. *Settlement and the Mining Frontier* appeared finally in 1936; but there was still an immense amount of work to be done on his study of the cod fisheries; and, with his usual impatience to push his great programme forward, he was taking on fresh commitments before he had finally discharged the old. He had agreed to edit the diary of James A. McPhail, the leader of the Wheat Pool during the days of the triumphs and final collapse of the Central Sales Agency. Part of July was spent in Winnipeg and Regina, inspecting the diary and interviewing McPhail's relatives and Wheat Pool officials; and then in August, came another of his many visits to Newfoundland. He was writing important articles for the *Journal*, doing a prodigious amount of reviewing, and superintending the final preparation of the first half dozen volumes in the Canadian-American Relations series. There were introductions to be written for *The Dairy Industry in Canada* and *Labour in Canadian-American Relations*. There was manuscript or proof of the studies by Lower, Glazebrook, and Creighton to be commented upon and corrected. It would have been far too heavy a burden for any ordinary person. In the end it was too much even for him. The late winter of 1937 brought the collapse which others had dreaded so long; and he spent most of March in bed, prostrate with nervous exhaustion.

It was ominous for the future. There was no prospect of a diminution of his responsibilities or a decline in the driving urgency of his purpose. And in July, 1937, he reached the top of the academic ladder up which he had begun to climb in 1920. E. J. Urwick retired from academic life; and Innis was appointed Head of the Department of Political Economy at the University of Toronto.

CHAPTER THREE

I

THE SIGNIFICANT PERIODS in Innis's career were periods of ten years, which coincided nearly, if not exactly, with the decades of the century. In 1920, he had presented his thesis on the Canadian Pacific Railway to the Graduate School of the University of Chicago. His first great work, *The Fur Trade in Canada*, was published in 1930; and in 1940, exactly ten years later, the *Cod Fisheries: The History of an International Economy*, was to appear. Since Innis's own scholarly research was so enormously important to him, the dates of the publication of these books were for that very reason of prime significance. They marked the end of long, laborious, and exciting investigations; they witnessed, in each case, the beginning of a new venture into some vast, unexplored, and inviting territory. These terminations and commencements of research were of the utmost importance. And yet they did not quite exhaust the significance of the ten-year period in Innis's career. The ten-year period had another and a more general meaning. It saw, in each case, a change in Innis's general interests, an enlargement of his role in the academic world, a lifting of his intellectual horizon. In the 1920's, he had been a solitary scholar; he had grown to be a prominent authority on the Canadian economy during the 1930's; and, in the decade that was now approaching, he was to become a university statesman and a student of world affairs.

The fact that these major stages in Innis's career happened to coincide with the decades of the century was a circumstance of more than merely passing interest. In part, of course, the coincidence was purely accidental; but, in another and very important way, it was not. In the world in which Innis was simply an insignificant and helpless individual, the decades also had their own, enormously enhanced importance. The end, and the beginning, of each ten-year period was charged, sometimes with propitious, but more often with sinister, significance. In 1919, while Innis was toiling over the first chapters of his thesis, the post-war world of the Paris Peace Treaties was just beginning its brief, uneasy career. In 1929, at a time when the stock market crash was slowly deepening into the great depression, the last revision of the *Fur Trade in Canada* had just got nicely under way. And in 1939, while Innis was putting the final touches to the vast, complex manuscript of the *Cod Fisheries*, the war, which was to affect the university world as profoundly as it affected everything else, had just broken out.

These precise coincidences were, of course, fortuitous; but the general character of Innis's development during each ten-year stage of his career was influenced, in a curiously intimate fashion, by the dominant trend of the corresponding decade in world affairs. The 1920's—that last decade of security—had permitted him a brief period of scholarly isolation. The 1930's, with their long, bitter years of depression and frustration, had forced him into Canadian national affairs. The 1940's, which began in a desperate grapple and ended in a cold war, compelled him to look outward over the huge disturbed landscape of world politics. These, to be sure, were the natural, perhaps inevitable, responses to the invitations and compulsions of history; but, at the same time, the relationship between Innis's development and the onward march of the decades touched a deeper level of intimacy and subtlety. *The Fur Trade in Canada* was an essay in Canadian economic history. *The Cod Fisheries*, as its subtitle clearly indicated, was a study in international economic rivalries. The work of the 1940's was to have a wider range in space and a greater depth in time. It was to be, in fact, an investigation into the economic foundations of culture throughout a long succession of civilizations.

The two years which elapsed after Innis's appointment to the headship of the Department of Political Economy have thus, for small as well as big reasons, the curious quality which belongs to the end of an epoch. The twenty years of uncertain peace were dwindling away into the certain catastrophe of war. The sense of impending crisis was in the air like a gathering darkness. And yet, of course, this feeling of the inexorable approach of the end of things was not, in Innis's mind, the only sensation which made 1938 and 1939 seem years of final conclusions and fresh beginnings. The business of the decade—of a good deal more than the decade—was being wound up; and, as an historian, he was very conscious of the firm punctuation marks of history. He had achieved one of his greatest ambitions. He had been made Head of the Department. His senior colleagues—Urwick, McIver, Jackson, and Jackman—had either resigned or retired; and obviously one of his first tasks, as Urwick's successor, was to pay honour to their work and to make provision for the gaps which had been left by their departure. He edited *Essays in Political Economy in Honour of E. J. Urwick* which was published in 1938. *Essays in Transportation in Honour of W. T. Jackman*, also under his editorship, appeared a few years later, in 1941. In 1938 it was fifty years since Sir William Ashley had given his inaugural lecture as

Professor of Political Economy in the University of Toronto; and Innis decided that the fiftieth anniversary of the founding of the Department should be celebrated by a series of public lectures on important Canadian scholars, past and present, to which he himself contributed a paper on Stephen Leacock. The past—and its principal figures—was thus suitably honoured. He could turn to the present and future. Two senior scholars, R. M. Dawson of the University of Saskatchewan and H. A. Logan of the University of Western Ontario, accepted his invitation to join the Department at Toronto.

Outside the University, in the world of Canadian scholarship as a whole, the same process was taking place. New projects were already under consideration. The great collective enterprises of the 1930's were being rapidly brought to a conclusion. The new generation of Canadian scholars, some of whom were Innis's contemporaries and some his older students, were making their final statements about a Canada which was to disappear completely and irrevocably with the coming of the second great war. In 1938 Innis contributed an introduction to G. P. de T. Glazebrook's *A History of Transportation in Canada* and an editorial preface to A. R. M. Lower's *The North American Assault on the Canadian Forest*. The last volumes in *Canadian Frontiers of Settlement* were published; the final studies in *The Relations of Canada and the United States* series were nearly ready to go to press. Even that elaborate, anxious investigation into the workings of Canadian federalism, which had been encouraged and sponsored by the Canadian Political Science Association and by the *Journal*, and to which so many economists, political scientists, and historians had contributed, was now having its final fruits in the vast comprehensive research programme of the Royal Commission on Dominion-Provincial Relations. Innis, of course, made no direct contribution to the work of the Commission; but its long list of scholarly studies, which was without parallel in any earlier governmental investigation, would have been quite impossible to carry out if it had not been for the research which he and Mackintosh had undertaken and encouraged, and the students they had trained during the previous decades.

In the meantime, while all this was going on, Innis was rounding out to its completion the last ten years of his own work. He was as busy, at least during term time, as he had ever been; but, perhaps a tacit admission of the gravity of his breakdown in the late winter of 1937, the summers were not quite so breathlessly crammed with restless wanderings as they had been in earlier years. It was true that in August, 1937, he went to England to attend the meeting of the British Association, and that in June of the following year he travelled east to Orono, Maine, for a conference, sponsored again by Shotwell and the Carnegie Endowment for International Peace, on education in Canadian-American Relations. But these were brief, unadventurous forays in comparison with the gruelling forced marches of the past. Satisfied, at least temporarily, with his detailed, panoramic knowledge of the whole of Canada, he almost seemed to be settling down. He took some, if not a great many, holidays during the summer, He rented a cottage in the Muskoka region, north of Gravenhurst, where a great many members of Ontario universities had long possessed summer places and where he and his family had never gone before except for brief visits. Other professors spent whole summers or whole months in Muskoka; and, although Innis could not quite bring himself to follow this generous example, he found more time than ever before for contented summer relaxation with his family and his friends. His visits to Foote's Bay, on Lake Joseph, were not usually very prolonged; and with him, in his bulging dispatch case, there invariably travelled books, papers, manuscripts, or proofs. Yet, with frequent week-ends and a few longer holiday periods, he managed to spend a fair amount of the summer in the north. He boated and picknicked with his children; there were almost always visitors, and good talk and stories during the long summer evenings.

During the winter of 1937, he had sent the bulk of the manuscript of the *Cod Fisheries* down to Shotwell in New York. Shotwell congratulated him on "the the completion of a fundamental contribution to our knowledge"; and Brebner, who read the work during the following summer, described it as a "magnificent achievement in scholarship". But it was obvious that a great deal would have to be done before the enormous, untidy manuscript was ready for the press. Innis himself, in his covering letter to Shotwell, had admitted that the last chapters—presumably those dealing with the period after 1833—were not yet in final shape; and to both Shotwell and Brebner it seemed clear that unless the difficulties and obscurities of the text were in some way corrected, they might seriously affect the value and prejudice the reception of the volume. It was difficult, exasperating work; and Innis was at his most ineffectual in the final stages of the preparation of a manuscript. His style was difficult, highly condensed, extremely elliptical, and not infrequently obscure. Long, none too obviously relevant quotations and big chunks of statistics were inserted, in a solidly unassimilated form, in the middle of his text. The steps which had led him from the immense detail of his evidence to the grand, sweeping generalizations of his conclusion were often most imperfectly indicated; and there were huge excrescences in the material and gaps and discontinuities in the argument which might only too easily bewilder and exasperate a reader. It had been true within limits—limits which Innis had always tried his best to narrow —of all his writings. It was perhaps more apparent in this volume, which was the largest he had ever produced. And in these first years of his headship of the Department, with scores of serious obligations and innumerable calls upon his time, he somehow felt incapable of giving the time and the patient effort which were necessary to push the manuscript through its final stages to completion. Shotwell tentatively suggested an editorial assistant; and Innis accepted the proposal. Arthur E. McFarlane, an ex-Canadian friend of Shotwell's, an admirer of Innis's work, and a writer who had considerable experience in preparing manuscript for the press, came up to Toronto to lend his assistance; and during the winter of 1938, he and Innis began, in collaboration, a thorough revision of the *Cod Fisheries*.

The work of the decade was drawing to a close. He had been made President of the Canadian Political Science Association immediately before his appointment to the headship of the Department at Toronto; and in May, 1938, his presidential address, "The Penetrative Powers of the Price System", was delivered at the annual meeting of the association in Ottawa. It was an attempt to draw together some of the implications, for economic theory, of his historical studies. His earlier work—particularly his writings on the Canadian fur trade—had stressed the importance of technology as a factor in economic change; the address to the Canadian Political Science Association modified this interpretation by an analysis of the historical significance of the price system. It was another, and an impressive, illustration of the essential independence of Innis's thought. His contemporaries, in Canada as elsewhere, had for some time been running with obsequious admiration after the highly fashionable figure of Keynes. Innis never joined this modish procession. His speculations were his own; and he disliked monopolies and dictatorships in economic and historical theory as much as he disliked them in real life. "I keep coming back," he wrote later to Joseph Willits of the Rockefeller Foundation, "to my own particular interests in what I laughingly call 'research', namely the persistent tendency in the field of knowledge and in the social sciences to build up monopoly or oligopoly situations. The literature builds up around the name of Keynes or Marx or someone else and everything else is dropped. A situation responsible for these tendencies is dangerous and comes a little short of dictatorship. . . . What I am wondering about is whether we can reach a position in which there is continuous discussion of vital problems. Problems cease when they become unmanageable or monopolies. . . ."

His own conclusions had grown naturally out of his immensely detailed researches in Canadian economic history. He had, in fact, become the greatest Canadian national historian. Yet no historian was less affected than he by the prepossessions and assumptions of the popular nationalist school of the 1930's. His work had been done in complete independence of its fashionable views; his conclusions exactly contradicted some of its pet theories. The nationalists—it was their proudest boast and dearest principle—had insisted upon the essential North Americanism of Canada. Planted solidly and aggressively upon the free soil of the continent, they defied the imperialism of Europe and welcomed the comradeship of North America. For them the one really serious struggle which Canada had ever had to wage was the struggle to win autonomy inside the British Empire; and the achievement and maintenance of a separate political existence on the North American continent had been, in emphatic contrast, a facile, almost perfunctory affair. They blandly took Canada's survival in North America for granted, as something which had just occurred, not as something which had had to be won. In their view, the great, simple, single theme in the history of the Dominion was the conflict between Canadian nationality and British imperialism. The only appropriate subject for a respectable, right-thinking Canadian nationalist was the struggle by which Canadians had ascended from the degraded status of dependent colonialism to the serene eminence of autonomous nationhood.

The fact that a great many important aspects of Canadian history were unrelated to this beautiful fable or exactly contradicted it, did not greatly concern the nationalist Canadian historians. They did not feel too limited by the facts of Canadian history. They were interested in theories; and two currently fashionable revolutionary theories of historical development had impressed them deeply. One of these was, of course, the idea of the class struggle which the C.C.F. "brains trust", in their dutifully imitative fashion, had tried to introduce into Canadian historiography; the other was that homespun expression of the isolationism of the middle-western United States, the "Frontier Theory". The Frontier Theory, despite the earnest efforts of the League for Social Reconstruction to persuade people that it was a backward-looking philosophy, "which ignored the fundamental trends of capitalist development", was, on the whole, much the more popular of the two with the nationalists. They liked the Frontier Theory. It was so thoroughly North American, so gratifyingly isolationist. It denied the old view that the movement of western civilization had been outward from its historic home in Western Europe; it insisted that the source of inspiration and action was to be found not at the centre, but at the periphery, of western culture. The frontier, "the hither edge of free land", was "the greatest formative influence" in Canadian, as in American, history.

To almost all of this Innis was fundamentally opposed. His two greatest works in Canadian economic history, the *Fur Trade* and the *Cod Fisheries*, completely undermined the basic assumptions upon which the whole nationalist philosophy rested. The *Fur Trade* broke down the conception of the North American continent as a geographical unit, an undivided whole; the *Cod Fisheries* invalidated the notion of the isolation of North America from Europe. Innis conceived of the new continent as inevitably and inextricably bound up with the political conflicts, the economic rivalries, the cultural cross-currents of West European–American civilization as a whole. He believed that Canada in particular had been deeply dependent upon the markets, political power, and military assistance of Europe, precisely because Canada had been determined to maintain, as the real essence of its being, a separate and competitive position in North America. The Dominion—it was the great discovery upon which the whole argument of his *Fur Trade* was based—was not simply an unrelated series of northern projections of the main economic regions of the United States. On the contrary, its economic axis was a great competitive east-west trading system, founded on the St. Lawrence River and the Great Lakes, one end of which lay in the metropolitan centres of western Europe and the other in the hinterland of North America. It was a transoceanic as well as a transcontinental system; and from Europe, from both France and Great Britain, had come the men, the capital, and goods—the ideas, institutions, and creative power—by which Canada had been enabled to maintain its identity and its separateness in the new world.

In the warm, sunny June of 1939, when Innis rode down to Canton, New York, for the third Conference on Canadian–American Relations, the long labour of the revision of the *Cod Fisheries* was almost finished. He was reading proof at the cottage at Foote's Bay during much of the latter part of August; and the index, which he commenced before the month was out, was completed on September 17, just one week after Canada declared war against Germany. It was the most curiously exact of all the coincidences of his career. At the very moment when his second great book was finished, when, as it turned out, the overwhelming bulk of his work in Canadian economic history was done and ended, the world was flung suddenly into the most appalling military struggle in its history.

III

Innis had watched the approach of war with the greatest anxiety; he marked its advent with apprehension and dismay. His whole attitude to it was deeply and darkly coloured by his experiences in the War of 1914–18. He had fought through one of the greatest battles of that war as a private soldier; he had received a wound which had partly crippled him for seven long years of his life; and the memory of the blood and mud and hunger and danger, which he and thousands of other simple country boys and town workers had endured in common together, came back now in a violent gush of feeling. He viewed this war—he viewed all wars—with the eye of a man in the ranks. Instinctively and unconsciously, he cherished the loyalties, resentments, and hatreds of the private soldier. His highly individualistic philosphy had always kept him sceptical and critical of power and authority even in peace time; but the power and authority appropriate to war he regarded with frank and unconcealed dislike. Military high command was bad enough; but worse—infinitely, insupportably worse—were the supervision and direction exercised by civilian "war-workers" safely ensconced in comfortable offices on Parliament Hill in Ottawa and Whitehall in London.

His opinion of such "war-workers" was simple and unqualified. He regarded them as contemptible beings. He suspected that a good many estimable people would consider this view to be blind, unreasoning prejudice; but he had not the slightest intention of attempting to change or qualify it. "My views," he wrote frankly to Arthur Cole, the economic historian, "are undoubtedly biased, and are those of a casualty wounded and invalided out of the last war. After eight months of the mud and lice and rats of France, in which much of the time was spent cursing government officials in Ottawa, I have without doubt developed an abnormal slant. I have never had the slightest interest since that time in people who were helping in the war with a job in Ottawa or in London. The contrast between their method of living and France simply made it impossible for me to regard them as having anything to do with the war and I continued to look on them with contempt. This of course is unreasonable but there it is."

There it was indeed. And there, without any doubt, lay a part at least of the explanation of the course of conduct which he followed so steadfastly during the next few years. Military service was, for him, impossible; and service in one of the numerous wartime boards and commissions, which flourished in such a prodigal fashion and swallowed up so many of his willing fellow-economists and political scientists, was completely abhorrent to him. He would stay with the University. The university tradition, the tradition of scholarship, of learning and teaching, was a vitally essential element of western civilization. If the war meant anything, it meant the defence of such a tradition. And if the preservation of this inheritance was accepted as a prime object of the conflict, then the first duty of the members of the university community was to maintain it, intact and unimpaired, in all the vigour of its original vitality, until the war was over. They owed this to society; they owed it to posterity; they owed it, above all, to the young men who had gone off to fight in the war and who —some of them at least—would be coming back gratefully and eagerly to the universities when it was over "When I came back in the spring of 1918 to do graduate work," Innis explained to Arthur Cole, "I found the universities depleted of staff in Canada and at Chicago in the United States, because people were bustling back and forth winning the war, they said, or their friends said. This meant of course that after taking the dirt in France I was expected to take more dirt when I came back from people whom I regarded with contempt. The point of all this is that I determined never to have any part in letting men down who had been in the front lines. It is that attitude and the attitude of men in the government when Canada entered the war who had had similar experience that led them to insist that as far as possible educational institutions must carry on."

During the next few years, he was to become one of the stoutest defenders of the university tradition in Canada. The first wartime duty of the members of Canadian universities, he firmly believed, was to close their ranks and stick by their posts. They should keep up their research, continue their publications, carry on with the meetings of their learned societies, and maintain their scholarly standards in all possible ways. He had shown his high and jealous regard for those standards often enough in the past; and just before the war opened he had proved once again what embarrassingly firm action he was prepared to take in their defence. In April, 1939, he learnt in advance that the Lorne Pierce medal, awarded by the Royal Society of Canada for an outstanding contribution to Canadian literature, was to be given that year to Colonel Wilfrid Bovey, the author of *Canadien*. Innis was perfectly ready to agree that Bovey's writings had helped to improve English-speaking and French-speaking relations in Canada; but he was not prepared to admit that they had brought conspicuous distinction to Canadian literature. " . . . I am compelled," he wrote to the honorary secretary of the Society, "to make a determined protest. . . . I have decided to submit herewith my resignation to the Royal Society and, of course, to the position as secretary of Section II, to take effect when Colonel Bovey's selection for the medal has been ratified by the Society." To the consternation, embarrassment, and regret of everybody concerned, Innis's resignation stood; and it was not until the following year, when the regulations for the award of the Society's medals had been considerably revised, that he consented to take his place again among his fellows.

It was in this determined and uncompromising spirit that Innis prepared for the defence of scholarship in time of war. Academic standards, academic freedom, the right—and, indeed, the obligation—of scholars to carry on their traditional activities, in their accustomed ways, without interruption or interference—these were the principles upon which he was prepared to stand. When F. H. Underhill—with whom, as he admitted, he had often "crossed swords" in the past—was threatened with dismissal from the University of Toronto for writings and utterances which had, in wartime, become extremely offensive to many, Innis uttered a strong protest on his behalf. When the officers of various learned societies of which he was a member suggested that in a time of crisis the activities of such bodies had become of "minor importance" and might be curtailed or eliminated, Innis replied indignantly that "scientific meetings are not in the same category as commercial meetings and conventions and are essential to the maintenance of morale and the continuation of educational work". There were those, finally, who insisted that the social scientist should now forsake his traditional academic studies and throw himself into active participation in the making of the post-war world. Innis disliked and dismissed these appeals for precisely the same reason that he had rejected similar exhortations during the depression. "Social scientists who participated in active service in the last war," he declared emphatically, "have little excuse for forgetting either the lessons of the war or of the peace. They have no excuse for ignoring the contributions of Adam Smith and his successors as to the significance of division of labour. The social scientist will do well, and he cannot do better than, to follow the advice of his masters and specialize on his own interests. In other words he can make his most effective contribution to the maintenance of morale on the home front, to the advancement of his interests, and to the solution of the problems of democracy by showing confidence in the traditions of his subject and by minding his own business. He must either do this or throw in his hand to the enemy. . . . It is the scholar, more than any other, who must demonstrate to his colleagues and his students the necessity of continuous, active, mental alertness in facing the difficulties of his work, particularly in the social sciences. He must face the necessity of giving his life to the pursuit of truth and realize that he cannot hope to make contributions of significance with less than twenty to twenty-five years of his life and before he reaches an age of at least fifty. . . . He owes this to the traditions of scholarship, of universities, and of western civilization."

This, of course, was no mere empty moralizing. His preaching was simply a literal description of his own practice. Late in February, 1940, the *Cod Fisheries* was published; and within a few months he was deep in the new and vast subject which was to occupy him for the next ten years. Travel far afield was difficult, if not impossible, during the war; he had finished his giant perambulations in North America; and the early summers of the 1940's were relatively quiet, tranquil periods, filled with omnivorous and far-ranging reading. In June, 1941, he left for Palo Alto, California, to lecture in the Summer School at Leland Stanford; but much of the long vacations of 1940 and 1942 was spent at Foote's Bay, in Muskoka, and in 1943 he and his family stayed for a month at L'Islet, in Quebec Province. All this time he was pushing further and further into the vast, ramifying network of the newsprint industry and journalism. It was a subject which had, of course, interested him for years. The production on a grand scale of pulp and paper was an obvious stage in the wood trade; and the wood trade, beginning with square timber, deals, and sawn lumber, had been for generations one of the major Canadian staple trades. A. R. M. Lower, in the *North American Assault on the Canadian Forest* and in his other writings, had dealt effectively with the earlier phases of the history of the staple; but Innis concentrated on its later developments and, in the early stages of the Carnegie project, *The Relations of Canada and the United States*, he had considered contributing a volume on the Canadian pulp and paper industry.

He had not done so. The *Cod Fisheries* had replaced the earlier project. But, once the *Cod Fisheries* was published, he began gradually to appreciate the enormous importance and infinite possibilities of the subject which now lay ahead. The Canadian newsprint industry, as such, he fairly quickly mastered; it could be dealt with satisfactorily, through the now familiar approach, as a staple industry. But immediately beyond the manufacture of pulp and paper lay the strange and different world of journalism and the newspaper; and obviously the main stages in its modern industrial development, so far as the English-speaking world was concerned, had taken place not in Canada, but in Great Britain and the United States. He began to devour prodigous quantities of books—monographs, memoirs, biographies, autobiographies—on paper, printing, journalism, the book trade, censorship, and advertising. As early as the autumn of 1942, the first results of these labours took shape in an article called "The Newspaper in Economic Development", which appeared in the new *Journal of Economic History*. Already he had reached the firm conclusion that the press had been an extremely potent influence in economic and social change; and his paper traced the expanding consequences of the main developments in paper-making and printing during the industrial age. But behind the industrial age lay the earlier, pre-industrial periods. Behind the newspaper and the book were the vestiges of other, earlier forms of communication. And behind the civilization of Western Europe and America stretched a procession of older and vanished empires.

During these same years, while his own researches were carrying him far afield in space, and backward in time, he gave a good deal of thought and effort to the encouragement and promotion of research in general. The first lustrum of the 1940's—five years dominated by the greatest war in history— might very naturally have witnessed a decline in the scholarship in which he was most interested; but, on the contrary— and thanks in very large measure to his own initiative and energy—the whole trend of events was definitely the other way. The early 1940's saw the launching, in both Canada and the United States, of new scholarly enterprises and new organizations for the advancement of the social sciences. The founding of the Economic History Association and the first appearance of the *Journal of Economic History* were events which helped to ensure the continuity and expansion of the kind of studies to which Innis was primarily attached. Though both the Association and the *Journal* were primarily American projects, he took part in the planning of each; and he became the Association's second president, in succession to Edwin F. Gay. During much the same period, he was deep in the counsels of the Committee on Research in Economic History, which had been sponsored by the Social Science Research Council of the United States. All these undertakings brought him into close contact with a growing number of American scholars—with Arthur H. Cole, the Chairman of the Committee on Research in Economic History, and with Anne Bezanson, Robert B. Warren, Earl J. Hamilton, and others.

In Canada, during the early years of the war, the unfulfilled requirements of scholarship were far more basic than they were in the United States. In the United States, organizations such as the Social Science Research Council, the Rockefeller Foundation and the Carnegie Corporation had all been actively engaged for some time in the encouragement and support of scholarship. But no comparable bodies, and no comparable sources of funds, existed in Canada. The Canadian Institute of International Affairs, through its research committee, had to some extent attempted to fill this gap, so far at least as the social sciences were concerned; and the *Canadian Economy and its Problems*, which Innis and Plumptre had edited, had appeared with the Institute's encouragement and support. But this assistance—and the help which some of the universities occasionally gave to the researches or the publications of some of the members of their own staffs—seemed to Innis to be lamentably insufficient. He vigorously supported the proposal, made originally by Dr. R. H. Coats, the Dominion Statistician, that a committee be established to promote and co-ordinate research in the social sciences in Canada; and he and R. G. Trotter, the historian, of Queen's University, were chiefly responsible for calling together a small group of people interested in the discussion of such a project in Ottawa in May of 1938. It was this body which decided to set up provisionally a Canadian Committee on Research in the Social Sciences; and after a preliminary survey of the state and requirements of Canadian scholarship in the social sciences, the provisional committee appointed Trotter and Innis to prepare a plan for a permanent organization. In September, 1940, the Canadian Social Science Research Council came officially into being.

This, however, though it was an important step, did not go nearly far enough. The Canadian Social Science Research Council, by its very title, was inhibited from giving any substantial direct aid to studies in the humanities; and, despite the preliminary survey of its own special field, the Council was only too well aware of the fact that it knew far too little of the strong and weak points, the deficiencies which must somehow be met, and the capacities which merited real encouragement, in Canadian scholarship. When, therefore, in the spring of 1943, Section II of the Royal Society of Canada proposed the formation of a similar national organization for research in the humanities, the Canadian Social Science Research Council generously agreed to underwrite its initial costs; and in May, 1944, the new sister organization, the

Humanities Research Council of Canada, held its first official session in Montreal. In the autumn of the same year, encouraged by a substantial grant from the Rockefeller Foundation, the new Council began a systematic and thorough investigation of the position of the humanities in the nation's universities and colleges; and two years later, the results of this survey were published in a printed report, *The Humanities in Canada*. In the meantime, J. B. Brebner, the ex-Canadian who had retained his old Canadian associations and who had had so much to do with the Carnegie series, *The Relations of Canada and the United States*, was persuaded to undertake a more general investigation into the state of Canadian scholarship. Innis was heartily in favour of this new survey, and of the widest possible broadening of its terms of reference. "I am not sure that Professor Brebner would agree to undertake it," he wrote to David T. Stevens of the Rockefeller Foundation, "but I know of no one who would be more acceptable, and of no opportunity which affords such great possibilities and which could have more appeal to him."

It was highly significant that these new organizations and undertakings had got under way during the war. In Innis's mind—and in the minds of many of those who took part in the founding of the two councils—this coincidence in time was the necessary consequence of a much deeper and more important relationship. The inquiries into the state of Canadian studies in the humanities and social sciences and the attempts to give organized support and encouragement to research were all part of the defence of Canadian scholarship in time of crisis. Throughout the country, all academic work was obviously under very considerable pressure during wartime; but obviously also the liberal arts—and particularly those studies in the humanities and social sciences which could not be claimed to have any direct connection with the war—stood in a peculiarly perilous position. From the first, Innis had argued that senior scholars in these subjects should regard it as their wartime duty to stick to their posts and continue their work. But it was, of course, equally necessary, for the future of such studies, that a sufficient number of students engaged in them should be permitted to complete their undergraduate courses, and to proceed to the M.A. degree. At first, under the man-power regulations of the Canadian armed services, this small continuing number was adequately protected; but in the autumn of 1942 it looked as though these regulations were likely to be drastically altered, and to the prejudice of the students in the liberal arts. Innis flung himself wholeheartedly into the defence of the liberal arts tradition; and he and Trotter were appointed a committee of two by the Canadian Social Science Research Council to draw up and present a memorandum on the whole subject to the Prime Minister of Canada, Mr. W. L. Mackenzie King. The memorandum quoted *Areopagitica*. It pleaded for the continuation of the liberal interpretation of the national selective service regulations. "The Arts tradition," it declared, "and particularly the strength of the Social Sciences, is the touchstone of democracy."

III

In the autumn of the year 1943, in which this memorandum was written, Innis received a most important letter from what was now called the Department of Economics at the University of Chicago. Chester W. Wright, who nearly twenty-five years before had been teaching Innis economic history at Chicago, was soon to retire from the Department. A new economic historian, of Wright's quality and stature, was required to succeed the older scholar; and who could it more appropriately be than the Canadian whom Wright himself regarded as "his most outstanding student"?

At that point, Innis was forty-nine years old. He had been a member of the Department of Political Economy at the University of Toronto for twenty-three years; he had been its head for six. He must have had, at intervals, at least a few invitations to go elsewhere. He had certainly threatened resignation and considered leaving at certain unhappy crises in his career. But, up to that moment, he had never received an academic offer of such obvious importance. He treated it with the grave courtesy which it deserved. He wrote expressing his gratification, and requesting further information about the proposed post. Late in December he travelled west to Chicago to discuss the offer in detail with the members of the Department of Economics. He found them ready and eager to meet his every difficulty and objection. They were willing to free him from all teaching in American economic history, or to work out a joint arrangement with the University of Toronto which would enable him to come to Chicago for at least a quarter each year. They were even prepared, as one of their members said later, "to give him *carte blanche* to work out his own plans for his connection with the University". And when Innis, pleased and touched by these repeated generosities, requested further time for consideration, the Chicago authorities were, they declared, only too delighted "to leave the door open" for a while yet.

"I have had no final word on the Chicago problem," he wrote to Edward Brown late in February, 1944. "I did finally write and turn the proposal down chiefly on the ground that I could not leave now and that I could not expect them to wait until the indefinite period here came to an end. They have returned to the question and it is again open, but not to be

117

decided in the immediate future." The immediate future was still dominated by the war and by the strains and stresses which it had imposed upon his own Department, his University, his students, and the studies and interests which had always been closest to him. It was true that, as 1944 drifted onward, the possible end of the war could be dimly discerned ahead. But it would probably be months, if not years, before the struggle was finally over; and further long years would undoubtedly have to pass before the student-veterans would all have finished their courses and gone out into the world. He could not possibly abandon these young men. He had preached loyalty to the Canadian scholars of the future. How could he, at this juncture of all others, desert the institution to which their largest numbers would certainly return? It was unthinkable for a while—for quite a while. But would it be equally unthinkable in a more distant future? He was a Canadian. He had struck thick and deep roots in the Canadian scene. His previous research had lain chiefly in Canadian history. His friends, his interests, his influence, his authority, were all Canadian. Could he give them up? "In ways difficult to describe," wrote a discerning friend, "transplantation to the United States is deceptively easy at first, but fairly shortly it involves odd unhappinesses and regrets which may or may not be comparable with the ones one would have experienced at home."

He could not depart at that particular moment. He began to suspect that it might be impossible for him ever to bring himself to go. The approaching influx of veterans would alone have kept him at his post; but, in addition, it was already obvious that the inevitable and enormous increase in the size of the student body was not the only major development which the post-war years were likely to bring to the University of Toronto. The first fresh stirrings of change were already in the air. The long reign of H. J. Cody, who, as Minister of Education, Chairman of the Board of Governors and President of the University of Toronto, had dominated higher education in the Province for so long, was now drawing to a close; and Sidney Smith, the ex-President of the University of Manitoba, who had come to Toronto first as Principal of University College, succeeded Cody as President of the University in 1945. The change from the political pressures and financial stringency of the war and pre-war years to the rapid expansion and unbounded confidence of the post-war period had thus coincided with a major change in academic leadership; and Smith, who was a great deal younger than his predecessor and who belonged, in fact, to Innis's own generation, was of a temperament and character to take instant and effective advantage of the favourable situation which he had inherited. He had a genuine passion for education, a broad understanding of the nature and needs of an academic community, a constant but critical interest in improvement and reform, and an abounding confidence and physical energy.

It was likely, Innis realized, that, for years to come, the University would be bustling with plans, reforms, investigations and academic enterprises of every conceivable kind; and he himself, as head of one of the largest and most important departments in the Faculty of Arts, was brought inevitably into the inner circle of the planning for reorganization and expansion. An Institute of Business Administration was established, with V. W. Bladen, now one of the senior professors in Political Economy, as its first Director. There was, for some time, a good deal of discussion of a proposed School of Journalism. And, finally, within eighteen months of Smith's accession to the presidency Innis was appointed chairman of a presidential committee empowered to inquire into the structure and operation of the School of Graduate Studies and to make recommendations for its reorganization and reform. There could be no conceivable doubt of his position now. He had reached the pinaccle of his influence and authority in Canadian university life. He had become Canada's senior academic statesman. His own University had gladly recognized his pre-eminence. It was accepted, apparently with equal cordiality, by the Canadian university world as a whole. The University of New Brunswick had given him an honorary degree in 1944; his old University, McMaster, paid him the same compliment in the following year. He occupied an absolutely unique position in the academic life of Canada. How could he give this up to become a late and reluctant emigrant to the United States?

All this was much. But there was something more as well. His own studies, the whole course of his intellectual development, was leading him further and further away from North America and deeper and deeper into an attitude of critical detachment from North American civilization. All during the later war years, he had steadily pursued his studies in communications, ancient and modern. He had come to understand the vastness of his new subject, though even yet some of its furthest implications were still hidden from him. He had never been a very orthodox economist. He was rapidly becoming sharply critical of the "present-mindedness" and specialization of modern economics; and he himself had set out on a lonely and difficult journey, by an unchartered route, into the most distant countries of the mind. At the centre of the study of communications, lay the problem of understanding among peoples of different cultures and ages. Innis insisted upon the necessity of the "broad approach". He valued, above everything else, the truth of synthesis. And he was driven inevitably into a stupendous comparative investigation of the interrelations of communications with politics, economics, and religion, throughout history and over the entire world.

Even this was not all. By the end of the war, he had ceased spiritually to be a North American. And, by a curious and significant coincidence, it was at this precise point that his overseas travel recommenced. The summer of 1944 had been spent, once again, in lecturing at the University of British Columbia. But these long, quiet, reflective wartime vacations, with their holidays in Quebec and northern Ontario, their voracious consumption of books and their lecture courses in California and British Columbia, had come to an end; and towards the close of May, 1945, barely three weeks after the war in Europe had ended, Innis received, from the Soviet Embassy in Ottawa, an invitation to be present at the celebration in Moscow and Leningrad of the 220th anniversary of the Academy of Sciences of the U.S.S.R. On June 6, with his two companion delegates to the Russian Conference, he set out from Ottawa in an R.C.A.F. plane. It was strange, north-west of Edmonton, to find himself travelling so swiftly and effortlessly over the empty, rugged country through which he had toiled on foot, and in canoes and small river steamers, twenty years ago. "Well," he wrote to Mary Innis on June 14, for they had missed a day in transferring to the Russian calendar, "we arrived yesterday afternoon about four o'clock—much greeting, and photographing, and finally taken to the Savoy Hotel where we have three adjoining rooms. . . . My ears are still buzzing after the trip yesterday afternoon. . . ."

It was only the briefest of visits. By July 4, he had reached Fairbanks, Alaska, on his journey home. But swift and impressionistic as it was, the experience had nevertheless had an immense impact upon him. "The whole venture," he wrote to Anne Bezanson, "was a tremendous shock to me. . . . It may seem ridiculous to think that Marx should be used to open up Russia to the industrial techniques of the West, but so it seems. I have felt the necessity for a much broader approach in economic history and the very great danger of a very narrow approach such as we seem to get nothing else but. Somehow we must work out approaches in the social sciences which will include the Russian situation now that it has become part of the West. I think I learned a little about the necessity of being tolerant and to be a little humiliated that I knew almost nothing about the situation. . . ."

The sense of a new world, which had just been discovered and must be understood, was overwhelming. Once again, as so often before in his career, the experience of travel had enlarged and clarified the enlightenment of his reading. He felt, as he had felt very rarely in the past, that he had something of immediate importance which must be communicated to the mass of his fellow-citizens. He was—it was almost a preposterous role for him—a man with a message; and the passage of time would only serve to bring out, with more disturbing clarity, how ironically, how tragically appropriate his message was. At the very moment when his journey to Moscow was undertaken, the brief concord, born of the war, between Russia and the English-speaking world had already entered upon its rapid process of disintegration; and within two years, the West, of which the United States had pugnaciously taken over the leadership, was confronting Russia and the East in the unseeing and implacable hostility of the Cold War. It was almost as if, in anticipation of an event which he may have dreaded and which he never ceased to lament, Innis resorted to methods which, for him, were efforts of publicity, almost of propaganda. His Russian diary, divided in two instalments and followed by a third article in which his impressions and conclusions were summed up, was published in the *Financial Post*; and during the autumn and winter of 1945–46, he spoke repeatedly to groups and societies on his experiences in the Soviet Union. "The major problem of the West," he wrote in the *Financial Post*, "is therefore co-operation between Russia and the Anglo-Saxon world. ... To establish contact, a common world view is today more essential than ever."

The war was over now. The post-war problems which everybody had been anticipating and dreading for so long, had assumed the formidable shapes of actuality; and the University of Toronto was straining to accommodate itself to a torrential influx of student veterans. Innis was wearied with administrative duties, critical of the current popular tendencies in his profession of economics, doubtful of or impatient with some of the recent developments in Canadian university life, and increasingly opposed to the drift of world politics and the deepening division between West and East. "Yes!" he wrote with somewhat tired cynicism to Anne Bezanson, "we have a new batch of presidents practically completed. I wish I could make up my mind about the role of a president. Brebner's report has something to say about scholars and he reaches the real point that Canada has never really had a place for them. In my more depressed moods I am wondering whether we will ever have a place for them. But I have still not yielded to Chicago. ... " He had still not yielded to Chicago; but Chicago had by no means abandoned its pursuit of him. During June and July, 1946, he went for three weeks to lecture in the University of Chicago Summer School; and it was at this time that the offer, which had been made originally nearly three years before, was renewed in terms even more generously liberal. He was invited to accept a professorship in the Division of Social Sciences, without any obligations to the Department of Economics or to any other unit in the university except the Committee on Social Thought. "You would be free," the letter of invitation carefully explained, "to develop your scholarly work here exactly as you choose, without any specific teaching obligations." It was an extremely attractive proposal. It was perhaps particularly attractive to a man who had already, in good measure, done his stint for Canadian history, Canadian economics, and Canadian academic institutions, and who was now venturing far beyond Canada in time and space into remote realms of speculation about which most of his incurious colleagues and associates knew little and cared less.

Yet he still delayed. And while he delayed and apparently hesitated, he was all the time becoming more deeply involved in Canadian activities, more embarrassingly loaded with Canadian honours and rewards, more heavily committed to Canadian plans and projects which would take years or decades to work out to a satisfactory completion. In May, 1946, he was elected President of the Royal Society of Canada. Earlier in the year, he had accepted a position on the Royal Commission on Adult Education, set up by the Province of Manitoba, with Dr. A. W. Trueman, the President of the University of Manitoba, as its chairman; and on a number of occasions during the year he travelled west to Winnipeg to hear and digest submissions and evidence and to discuss with his fellow-commissioners the framing of their report. In the meantime, the expansion and reorganization of the University of Toronto was proceeding apace; and the presidential committee on the reconstruction of the Graduate School, of which he was the chairman, stuck closely to its task all during the winter of 1946–47. Innis was deeply interested in the making of these plans. An organization which would train the scholars of the future, which would encourage the pursuit of truth on the highest levels of inquiry and speculation was, in his view, a centrally necessary feature of the "university tradition".

How could he cut himself loose from all these Canadian engagements, present and future? His loyalty to Canada—embarrassed, critical, impatient, yet defiantly irrepressible—remained. He told a friend that he did not believe his mother would ever forgive him if he deserted Canada. He perhaps had never seriously faced the question whether he would be able to forgive himself. And all the while, as the year 1947 drew on, and as the international suspicions and rivalries of the first post-war years hardened rapidly into the implacable animosities of the Cold War, his own affection for Canada was being steadily strengthened by a mounting dislike of the attitudes and policies of the United States. The United States, which had issued out of revolution, was now apparently reconstituting itself as a bastion of reaction against the disturbances of an impoverished, distressed, and agitated world; and having pre-empted the leadership of an uneasy and reluctant Europe and America, it confidently expected its followers—and of course particularly the Canadians—to stand up and be counted as the conscripts of a just cause. "I am afraid," Innis wrote to Gerald Graham in the spring of 1947, "that I share to some extent the views that our foreign policy is determined by Mr. Truman's views about being elected for a second term. I am afraid we are in for trouble since the United States has never faced in a big way the problems of imperialism before. Consequently they have fallen back upon the military with results which are to be expected. One day we shall have the Roman Catholic Church and the French

Canadians attempting to conscript us to fight Russia. But that, I hope, will be in the distant future."

In the spring and early summer of 1947 all these uncertainties were ended. There was, after all, to be no sharp turn in the course of Innis's development. He accepted the University of Toronto's invitation to become the first Dean of its newly reorganized Graduate School; and this, in effect, brought the long drawn out negotiations with Chicago to a final close. It was not the United States, but—by an odd chance—England, which was to be the scene of some of his major appearances as a scholar during the next few years. Twelve months earlier, in June, 1946, the administrators of the Beit Fund at the University of Oxford had requested him to give six lectures "on any subject in the economic history of the British Empire". He had agreed to deliver the Beit Lectures in the Trinity Term of 1948; and he subsequently accepted invitations to give the Stamp Memorial Lecture at the University of London and the Cust Foundation Lecture at the University of Nottingham during his visit to England in the early summer of 1948. He had not changed his direction, but confirmed it. There was even, in the acceptance of these important scholarly commitments, a slight, symbolic suggestion of a veering away from the United States and a return to Canada's deepest and most important political and spiritual connection. He would stay with his old University, and his native country, and his native country's oldest allies. He would do Canada's work and be satisfied with Canada's honours. These honours were coming thicker and faster now, as the whole nation acknowledged his eminence; and, in the spring of 1947, an eastern and a western institution, Laval University and the University of Manitoba, conferred on him their honorary degrees.

There was one further significant development in the spring

of 1947. Late in May, at Quebec City, he delivered his presidential address, entitled "Minerva's Owl", to the Royal Society of Canada. The paper was much too long; and, as if its author were unhappily conscious of his prolixity, the whole, detailed, highly condensed argument was read in a most hurried and unemphatic fashion. Many in his audience were puzzled or bewildered; but, despite these imperfections in its delivery and reception, "Minerva's Owl" was perhaps the most important general statement of the last phase of Innis's career. It was a great general conspectus, viewed from the top of the high hill to which he had painfully climbed, of the comparative study, through half a dozen different civilizations, of communications as the economic foundations of culture. He was to spend the last five years of his life in completing the work for which "Minerva's Owl" had presented the prolegomena.

IV

During the academic year 1947-48, the post-war population at the University reached the high mark of its flood-tide. Innis sat in the small, dingy, irregularly shaped room with the tall, narrow windows which was his office in the Economics Building at 273 Bloor Street West, and tried to cope with the thousand pressing details of university administration. There was an enormous amount of work to do. He was Head of the Department of Political Economy, which had always been one of the most popular departments in the Faculty of Arts, and Dean of the reorganized Graduate School, which began to grow rapidly in consequence after the conclusion of the war. He had accepted both these tasks willingly, as a matter of right and a matter of duty. It was one of his strongest convictions that a university, in order to preserve its essential character and to safeguard its fundamental purpose, must be governed, not by professional administrators, but by scholars. University administration, just as much as research, was part of a scholar's job. University administration was, in fact, a special kind of administration, which only a scholar could carry out. He saw no reason whatever to apologize for the fact that his own rule met few abstract principles of politics and conformed to still fewer canons of business efficiency.

He was very much the head of his department; and his leadership, relatively uninfluenced by the pressure of departmental routines, was a direct, almost unqualified expression of his own character and personality. He was tolerant of other people, sympathetic to their interests, sensitive to their rights, and disposed, once he had decided to give them a task or a responsibility, to let them carry it out, without interference, in their own way. He consulted his colleagues fairly widely; but the formal departmental meeting, with its invitations to endless argument and its premiums for oratory, was something which he did not particularly like and did not frequently call. He preferred to deal with individuals rather than groups and with particular problems rather than with administrative categories; and his approach tended to be selective rather than comprehensive and intuitive rather than strictly logical. The shelves which lined the walls of his small office were crowded with a dusty, ill-arranged collection of books and proof and manuscripts; the top of his desk was piled high with an untidy mass of letters, papers, and journals. The room might have seemed a shrine dedicated to disorder, delay, and inefficiency. Yet, for the things he valued, Innis was extremely alert and quick. The ease with which he could find the paper that he wanted and the swiftness with which he answered letters that he deemed important were surprising to many. He wrote most of his personal, and many departmental letters in longhand, partly because he could never get over the feeling that a dictated and typed communication was something of a discourtesy to its recipient, and partly because he strongly believed that the time of the departmental secretaries should not be given over completely to correspondence. In his view, the departmental secretaries should serve the Department's scholarship; and one of their most important functions was to type the books, articles, reviews, memoranda, and field notes which the members of the Department produced.

Throughout the University, he was becoming—had become —a character. His wry, ironic smile, his long, unruly lock of hair, his tall, slightly stooped figure, and swift, easy stride, made up a personality which, for whole hosts of students, stood out from his colleagues in arresting importance. He was not an immediately popular lecturer, with the easy, familiar, slightly slangy, and highly dramatic style which makes quick conquests among impressionable youths. He won his following later, when students had reached their senior years, and acquired a measure of discrimination, and were able to grasp something of the range of Innis's knowledge and the originality of his mind. He gave them of his best. His lectures were not stale, old exercises, written years ago, and dog's-eared through constant repetition. They were, on the contrary, reports of his most recent discoveries, first statements of his newest ideas, drafts of the essays and chapters which he hoped to publish in the near future. It was this exemplification of the constantly inquiring mind, of the ceaseless, untiring and undogmatic search for truth which was his first great gift to his students. He taught them to beware of "monopolies" and "oligopolies" of truth, of closed systems of knowledge, of the limitations of "present-mindedness" and parochial nationalism, of false appeals to utility and immediate application, and of the perils of specialization and quantitative measurement. In his judgment, the first and most necessary virtue of the inquirer was humility in the face of the boundless complexity of his subject matter. Yet, at the same time—and this was an equally important part of his creed—the student must not be intimidated into some narrow, specialized inquiry, contracted in both time and space. He must go forward on a "broad approach", through some significant synthesis, towards the recovery of the unity of knowledge.

The wisdom of Innis's teaching and his sure judgment on all basic questions of academic policy had made him a deeply respected, almost revered, figure in the University of Toronto. In the nation as a whole, his reputation as a scholar and his prestige as a wise statesman in everything relating to higher education had given him a position of acknowledged pre-eminence. In these first post-war years, he stood at the peak of his authority and influence. The place he had made for himself was unique. He had become the chief repository of academic information, the principal confidant of academic secrets, the accepted interpreter of academic opinion, and the final arbiter in academic disputes. In the university world, his knowledge and influence were quite exceptional; and, beyond the formal boundaries of the university domain, their range extended far into such neighbouring realms of thought and action as politics, administration, and business. His friends and acquaintances formed a very large and extremely varied company. Politicians, civil servants, journalists, manufacturers, labour leaders, farmers, prospectors, executives of the western co-operative movement, students and scholars of all disciplines and all ages, descended in a never-ending stream upon his office in the Economics Building and his house in Dunvegan Road. They brought information, retailed gossip, told stories, presented problems, outlined projects, solicited assistance, and begged advice.

He did all he could for them. He played his role superbly. He was good at it and he enjoyed it immensely. Every one of the long succession of visitors had his full attention, his earnest consideration, his best advice. He regarded their affairs with absorbed seriousness. And yet the fundamental gravity of his approach to the problems of the scholar and the university never weakened his amused interest in character, his ironic enjoyment of situations, his sheer delight in a good story or a good joke. For him the essential truth about a personality or a problem was often most completely contained and most suitably expressed in some absurd anecdote. He enjoyed stories. He was an indefatigable collector and connoisseur of stories; and they were brought to him in quantities from all over the country and by people in every walk of life. He had a special place in his interest and affection for friends and acquaintances who had a taste for irony, a gift for mimicry or comic exaggeration. He enjoyed the company of such visitors as politicians and journalists who brought with them a refreshingly different, urbanely cynical attitude to the comedy of men and circumstances. In his office or his study, with his long legs stretched out and his chair tilted back, he would exchange stories with unhurried delight; and the deep stream of his conversation rambled amiably through generous meanderings and over laughing shallows.

The crowded, busy session of 1947–48 came to an end mercifully early, for this was the year of his visit to England. The journey to Russia, three years before, had been the first journey outside North America which he had undertaken since the war began; and it was eleven years since he had visited Great Britain. When he and his wife set out from Toronto on the last day of April, it was with something even more exhilarating than a glad holiday feeling; it was with a sense of the impending rediscovery of a long-lost, and unquestionably ravaged, but still magically wonderful world. Spring had filled Oxford with the bloom and fragrance of flowers and blossoms, when, on May 12, he began his Beit Lectures in All Souls College. And despite his even more than usually crowded time-table and the fact that he was still working frantically on his incompleted lectures in England as well as on the Atlantic, the next few weeks were an agreeably exciting succession of engagements, appearances, honours, and travels. He spoke at Nottingham University and at the University of London. He attended the Commonwealth Universities Conference in Oxford; and late in July, the University of Glasgow gave him an honorary degree. There were a good many formal academic occasions; but he found time for unofficial visits to Cambridge, and Paris, and Devonshire, and the Isle of Man. He found time also, and lots of it, for long discussions on the state of England, Europe, and the world, with new English acquaintances and old English friends.

He came back with a greater suspicion and dislike than ever of the policies by which the United States was exacerbating the tensions of the Cold War. His journey had brought home to him the horror with which Great Britain and Western Europe faced the peril of being ground to pieces between the great primitive imperialistic power-blocs of Russia and the United States. "A visitor from North America to Great Britain and the continent," he wrote in the *Commerce Journal* in January, 1949, "can scarcely fail to sense a feeling of hostility. Much to his surprise he is regarded as coming from an area behind a gold curtain, and to find that he is in a sort of no man's land between iron and gold curtains. . . . A Canadian assumed to be an American finds attitudes perceptibly changing once it is understood that he is not an American. In a vague sense Canada probably appears to occupy a position in relation to the United States similar to that of Jugo-Slavia in relation to Russia, except that no Tito has appeared in Canada, but a Canadian visitor will sense a change of attitude reflected in greater frankness and in many cases savage criticism of the United States. . . . It is clear that European countries feel more directly exposed to American influence and that the threat of 'the cumulative advantage of size and technological progress' of the United States is in the impact of uniformity and standardization and its disastrous implications to the artistic culture of Europe and to western civilization."

There was another, related conviction which grew stronger during his visit to England and in the months after his return. He had come to believe firmly that Canada must remain between the iron curtain and the gold curtain and do what she could to sustain the European point of view. It was in her own interest, as well as in the interest of western civilization, for the Dominion to hold fast to the position of autonomy which she claimed in theory. But Innis was sceptical of Canada's power to resist the heavy weight of American propaganda and what he called the "crude effrontery of American imperialism"; and he even doubted whether the political leaders at Ottawa had any very great interest in making the attempt. "Pearson seems to be as active as possible in selling us down the river to the United States," he reported acidly to Gerald Graham in November. "It is hardly possible," he wrote in the *Commerce Journal* article, "for Canadians to understand the attitude of hostility because of the overwhelming influence of American propaganda, and even more difficult to strengthen the European point of view. . . . Whatever hope of continued autonomy

Canada may have in the future must depend on her success in withstanding American influence and assisting in the development of a third bloc designed to withstand the pressure of the United States and Russia, but there is little evidence that Canada is capable of these herculean efforts and much that she will continue to be justly regarded as an instrument of the United States."

The visit to England had enlarged his point of view and sharpened its focus. The Beit Lectures and the invitations to Nottingham and London had given him the opportunity of presenting a first, major report on his current researches and reflections. He did not feel himself to be limited or confined, in any serious way, by the terms of the trusts or funds under which he was invited to lecture. "If," he had once written to Arthur Cole concerning an applicant for research funds, "he is the type of mature scholar we want to encourage, he will have fastened on some subject from which we cannot detach him." He himself had no intention of being detached from the themes to which he had been giving most of his time and thought during the last few years. The Cust Lecture at Nottingham, which was supposed to be concerned with the British Commonwealth, gave him the opportunity for a caustically frank discussion of the relations of Great Britain, the United States, and Canada; and he used the Stamp Lecture, which was intended to have as its subject, "the application of economics or statistics to a practical problem or problems of general interest", as a vehicle for a witty and searching examination of the history of the Anglo-American press during the nineteenth century.

The Beit Lectures, six in number, were a more serious affair. The assignment obviously called for a more extended effort; and the terms of the fund required "a subject in the economic history of the British Empire". But Innis was no longer very interested in any subject which lay comfortably inside the economic history of the British Empire. The only major work which he had in contemplation was a history of the written and spoken word, not only in the British Empire, but also in Graeco-Roman civilization, and in the empires of Babylonia and Egypt. He may have tried, for a brief while at least, to accommodate himself more literally to the requirements of the Beit Fund; but this attempt was fairly quickly abandoned, and he decided to cram the essence of his long, elaborate historical argument on communications within the straining limits of six academic discourses. The attempt, of course, inevitably involved serious losses. His most comprehensive and original thesis was presented prematurely, too briefly, and without the vast mass of supporting evidence and illustrative material which otherwise he would almost certainly have included. He perhaps spoilt what would have been a bigger, and possibly a better, book. Yet there were gains as well as losses in the method of presentation which he had been forced to adopt. All the leading ideas of his new historical synthesis—the ideas of the oral tradition and the written tradition, of the communications which dominate space and the communications which survive time, of the necessary balance of these systems, and their influences in any vigorous and expanding empire—were all set out adequately in the lectures. And they were, moreover, presented with a simplicity, directness, and force, which recalled some of his best historical essays and the last great chapter of *The Fur Trade in Canada*.

V

It was during the winter of 1948–49, while the final revisions were being made in the manuscript that was to be published next year as *Empire and Communications*, that Innis was recalled from his study of vanished civilizations by a summons, peremptory and demanding, from the present world. He was invited, by the Dominion government, to become a member of a Royal Commission on Transportation, the chairman of which was to be the honourable W. F. Turgeon, High Commissioner for Canada in Eire, and the third member Professor H. F. Angus, of the Department of Economics, University of British Columbia. Innis decided to accept. It was a decision of major importance which affected all the remainder of his career. It had consequences, indirect but gravely serious, which developed only gradually over the next few years; and it produced an immediate and violent upheaval in Innis's university teaching and administration, in his reading and research, in the whole complex and congenial pattern of his scholarly pursuits. A Royal Commission on Transportation, established by the Dominion, was in no sense comparable with the Nova Scotian Royal Commission of Provincial Economic Inquiry on which he had served fifteen years before. The two differed, not in degree, but virtually in kind. The Nova Scotian inquiry had meant a brief inspection of one of the smallest provinces in the Dominion, and a few months' work in the late summer and autumn of the year. The federal investigation would require a systematic and protracted transcontinental tour, innumerable sittings, interminable technical argumentation, piles of elaborately detailed submissions, and months and probably years of work. All during the late winter and early spring of 1949, Innis travelled back and forward between Toronto and Ottawa. Towards the end of May, the Commission, with its formidable complement of counsel, secretaries, research assistants, press officers, and typists, began its western tour. Early in July, without any intermission, it set out for the eastern provinces; and late in September, after Newfoundland's entrance into Confederation had been effected, it paid a brief visit by aeroplane to the new island province. Long before this, Innis, who was probably one of the least patient of men under the constant reiteration of familiar views, had arrived at the point of satiation. "We are reaching the stage," he had written to Mary Innis as early as the sittings in Calgary, "when we hear very little that is new and much that is old stuff. As a result all of us are getting restive and anxious to get on. The lawyers are beginning to get on each other's nerves with noisy squabbling about this and that. It is really a lawyer's field day."

In the autumn, when the Commission's tours were finally ended, the Commissioners settled down in Ottawa to consider their evidence and discuss their findings. At that point Innis began what was probably the most uninterrupted and grinding labour of his entire career. It was obvious that he would have to stay in Ottawa for a considerable period of time. It would probably have been better if he had remained there continuously for several months at least. But he could not bear the thought of breaking his connection with the University for so much as even a single term. He could not bring himself to give up his students, the Department of Political Economy, the Graduate School, and all the activities and gossip of a great university. He had to be in Ottawa. He wanted to be in Toronto. And, with characteristic restless disregard for his own health and peace of mind, he devised a severely rigorous time-table which gave him the worst of these two disparate worlds. He usually spent the first five days of the week in Ottawa, travelling up to Toronto by the late afternoon train on Friday. On Saturday, there were undergraduate lectures, discussions with colleagues and senior students, correspondence, and visits to the Graduate School. Saturday evening and Sunday brought an all too brief period of recuperation and all too little time for visits with family and friends. And then, late on Sunday night, he boarded the train for Ottawa once more.

To make matters worse, he quickly became bored with Ottawa. "As I expected," he wrote to Gerald Graham in December, 1949, "I find Ottawa a place to stay away from; it is really very parochial and dull. . . . " While he was in the capital, he stuck fairly closely to his books and papers; he looked forward to his escape to Toronto at the end of every week. Official Ottawa, with its politicians, civil servants and diplomatic representatives, failed to provide him with the conversational relaxation and mental stimulus which he enjoyed so much; and he rapidly became tired of the air of mediocrity and the habit of intellectual submission which seemed to him so characteristic of the city. "I found Ottawa," he wrote to Gerald Graham, "especially the Department of External Affairs, very fatiguing—in fact exhausting. . . . There is very little intellectual atmosphere around the place, and one feels how much we have lost to the United States. We follow along and kid ourselves we are our own masters."

All this boredom and intellectual undernourishment did not help to mitigate the rigours of his ordeal. But there was, perhaps, a more fundamental disappointment in the work of the Royal Commission—a central emptiness which, in the nature of the task, could never be filled. During the last ten years his studies had led him further and further away from Canada into researches and speculations which, in his view, touched at the heart of modern problems, but which obviously did so in a general and philosophic fashion. He had been recalled abruptly to the here and now, the immediately practical. It was true that he had always been extremely interested in transportation; but he had viewed it, in the fashion which was invariably most congenial to him, as a permanent and important factor in Canada's historical development and not as a contemporary problem of enormous technical complexity. He had always been sharply critical of the evils of "present-mindedness" and he had taken delight in exposing the limitations of statistics and quantitative measurements. But the work of the Commission had plunged him back into a world whose spirit was strictly contemporary, whose approach to any problem was narrowly legal and mathematical, and whose favourite evidence and arguments were the massive and fatiguing products of an age of woodpulp and calculating machines. Innis did not feel at home in this kind of world or at ease in this kind of company. He probably did less than his best work in these circumstances. And on the whole, his acceptance of the appointment to the Commission may be regarded as a misfortune in that it delayed, and in the end prevented, the completion of studies which were both more congenial and more permanently valuable.

The postponement of his favourite studies was a major misfortune. But the deterioration of his health, which began before the Commission had finished its labours, was an ever-deepening tragedy. Late in 1948, before he had even accepted a place on the Commission, illness had kept him in bed for nearly a week; but from then on, for nearly eighteen long and wearying months of work, his health had apparently been reasonably good. He had successfully survived the fatigues of the transcontinental tours. The weeks of the autumn and winter had passed in a long and tiresome succession, each one bringing its journeys to and from Ottawa; and throughout he had scarcely ever varied his dismal routine. When the spring of 1950 broke, he was still plodding onward in this strict, closed circle of obligation; and then, when the composition of the *Report* had already begun and when, dimly ahead, the prospect of deliverance could be glimpsed, the hard blow fell. During the latter part of July, he became seriously ill. How far the fatigues and tensions of the work of the Commission may have encouraged the development of a disease which no doubt had older and deeper origins is a speculative question; but there was at least no doubt of the gravity of his condition. Early in September he went to hospital; and for some time after his return home he lay in bed, trying to keep up with his correspondence by dictation, and only gradually recuperating.

By this time, however, the inexorable demands of the Commission were coming to an end. Innis paid his last lengthy visit to Ottawa in December, 1950. The report was finished early in February, 1951; it was published about the middle of March; and, at long last, after two years of labour which had overtaxed his strength and monopolized his time, he was free once more to pick up his closest interests and favourite studies. He had never, of course, completely abandoned them. He had snatched time from railway statistics to do a little reviewing and to write an article or two. He had eagerly stolen away from the boring routine of Ottawa to attend the meetings of the learned societies in Canada and the United States. He had gladly availed himself of the invitation of the University of New Brunswick to participate in a lecture series commemorating its one hundred and fiftieth anniversary; and to this he had contributed two important papers on his old themes of communications, propaganda, and culture.

But these had been merely brief excursions from the land of bureaucracy, brief revisitations of the old world of scholarship. He was back for good now; but he was tired and worn by all he had been through, and even he was prepared to admit that before he would be able to take up his old affairs with any enthusiasm again, he very badly needed a holiday. Where could he go more happily than to England and Europe? And early in June he set out, with his younger son, Hugh, to cross the Atlantic again. There was a visit to Dublin to see W. F. Turgeon, the ex-Chairman of the Royal Commission on Transportation, who had now returned to his post as Canadian High Commissioner to Eire. There were the fifth centenary celebrations of Glasgow University to which Innis went as a representative of the University of Toronto; and a brief journey to Paris where he was invited to give an address at the Collège de France. In between these more formal occasions, he revisited old friends in Oxford, London, and Cambridge. As he told Gerald Graham, a visit to Britain "blew away the cobwebs" of the great empty barn that was North America; and when he got back again to Toronto, early in August, he seemed both physically recovered and spiritually refreshed. He took up his work in the University with what appeared to be his old vigour and enthusiasm. In the autumn he commenced a typical scholarly round of meetings and conventions at Princeton, Kingston, New Haven, and Philadelphia; and in December, at Boston, he was elected President of the American Economic Association.

In the meantime, he had returned to his studies. And in the years from 1950 to 1952 the contemporary implications of these studies for the world as a whole and for Canada in particular had grown ominously clear. He was led on, as he explained in the preface to *Changing Concepts of Time*, to develop his theories of communications "in relation to immediate problems". Two important events—completely unrelated in fact, yet curiously associated in his mind and in the minds of others —had compelled him to reflect "more sharply the temper of the period". The first of these two events was the outbreak of the Korean War in 1950, and the second was the publication, in 1951, of the Report of the Royal Commission on the Arts, Letters, and Sciences in Canada. The Massey Report, as it was called from its chairman, was the first thorough examination of the present state and future prospects of a distinct and different Canadian culture. The Report affirmed the value and promise of Canadianism. The Korean War, in sharp contrast, seemed to cast a doubt upon its validity. In the most explicit and challenging fashion, it appeared to call in question the whole conception of Canadian moral and intellectual independence—the very possibility for Canada, of anything but the most slavish submission to the interests and wishes of the United States. To Innis, the War in Korea seemed a transparently obvious adventure of American military imperialism in the Far East. But he soon discovered that in Ottawa these views were regarded with shocked expressions of outraged disapproval. In the East Block, the conflict was apparently accepted, at the mark-up which the United States chose to put upon it, as a great disinterested and altruistic crusade for the collective system; and the members of the Department of External Affairs and Ottawa officialdom in general applauded the "leadership" of the United States with all the uncompromising ardour of converts to a new religion. That supposedly intelligent people, whose trade was diplomacy, should show themselves at once so sanctimonious and so gullible, was, for Innis, a source both of entertainment and consternation. In his view, what had happened supplied one more incontrovertible proof that in wartime American propaganda became a battering-ram that flattened the last vestige of independent thought in Canada.

These anxious and indignant thoughts had informed the address which he gave at the University of Nottingham and the sesquicentennial lectures which he delivered at the University of New Brunswick. But in 1952 his apprehensions were given still more explicit and emphatic expression in two essays significantly entitled "The Strategy of Culture" and "Military Implications of the American Constitution". "With the entry of the United States into the Second World War," he wrote in "The Strategy of Culture", "instruments of propaganda were enormously extended. . . . The cultural life of English-speaking Canadians, subjected to a constant hammering from American commercialism, is increasingly separated from the cultural life of French-speaking Canadians. American influence on the latter is checked by the barrier of the French language but is much less hampered by visual media. . . . We are indeed fighting for our lives. The pernicious influence of American advertising reflected especially in the periodical press and the powerful persistent impact of commercialism have been evident in all the ramifications of Canadian life. The jackals of communication systems are constantly on the alert to destroy every vestige of sentiment towards Great Britain, holding it of no advantage if it threatens the omnipotence of American commercialism. This is to strike at the heart of cultural life in Canada. The pride taken in improving our status in the British Commonwealth of Nations has made it difficult for us to realize that our status on the North American continent is on the verge of disappearing. Continentalism assisted in the achievement of autonomy and has consequently become more dangerous. We can only survive by taking persistent action at strategic points against American imperialism in all its attractive guises. . . . "

VI

In Toronto, the winter of 1951–52 was particularly severe, with steady cold, lowering skies, and quantities of snow. And it was just at the dead point of midwinter, when the drifts in the road were deepest, that the employees of the Toronto Transportation Commission went on strike. In the early darkness of January evenings, Innis used to take the long walk up Avenue Road, towards his house on Dunvegan Road, stumbling along the rutted, uneven, partly cleared sidewalks, and carrying his despatch case, always heavily loaded, in his hand. When the pain is his back first came, he thought—or professed to think—that it was simply the result of some strain that he had incurred on these repeated and difficult walks. But the pain persisted, growing gradually worse. He had to take to his bed. And when, early in March, after an interval of some weeks, he reappeared in the University to introduce President Robert Hutchins, of the University of Chicago, as the Marfleet Lecturer for 1952, his friends and colleagues were shocked at the appalling change in his physical appearance. Only a few years earlier, when he had become President of the Royal Society, Gilbert Jackson had congratulated him on "the remarkable manner in which you have kept your youth". Now the compliment would have been a terrible mockery. His tall figure was gaunt and bowed; his untidy hair was nearly white; his face was pale and drawn with pain and exhaustion. Desperately, with the stoical courage of a man who, throughout his life, had virtually refused to recognize physical circumstances and had made whatever exorbitant demands upon himself his own designs seemed to call for, he tried, in the late winter and early spring, to carry on with his work. He appeared, rarely and briefly, at the University; he lectured, travelling to and from the Economics Building in a taxi, and going immediately to bed again on his return. And from his sick-room, with the aid of his secretary, he attempted, day after day, to keep up his correspondence, to superintend his

Department and the Graduate School, even getting himself entangled in a final dispute with the University authorities over a point of academic policy in which he was deeply interested. He tried to carry on. He summoned every ounce of will and purpose. But it was no use. The progress of his disease, the decline of his powers, continued with frightful rapidity. On April 17, he was taken to the Western Hospital. He was given a blood transfusion on April 21; and three weeks later, on May 14, the surgeons operated.

And then, after all the pain and struggle and effort of the past few months, there came a brief miraculous period of tranquillity. The cancer which was inexorably devouring his life had not been conquered. But it had been checked; it was held, for the moment, at bay; and for over two months, after his return from the hospital on May 31, he enjoyed what almost might have seemed a convalescence that would lead slowly but inevitably to complete recovery. The sunny summer days of June and July were warm and gently encouraging. A cot was wheeled out to the garden or the sun-room of his house; and there, in the pleasant mornings and afternoons, he lay, reading and dictating. He tried, at intervals, to prepare his presidential address for the American Economic Association; he began to dictate his memoirs; and every day brought its letters and its amusing conversations with the members of his family and visiting friends. His married daughter, Mary, came home with her baby; Donald, his elder son, returned from Europe; and while he still felt well and eager to talk, there was a constant procession of visitors. Andrew Gordon came to talk over the affairs of the Graduate School. Tom Easterbrook arrived every Friday morning to discuss a work in progress. George Ferguson of the *Montreal Star*, and Gerald Graham who happened to be that summer in North America, as well as

145

many of his colleagues and associates in the University, kept dropping in to see him for an hour or so.

In the latter part of August, this last bland, deceptive reprieve of his life drew towards its close. He was desperately ill again. There were two nurses in constant attendance; and although he rallied a little in September and was able to greet other friends and to enjoy other, almost gay conversations, the decline of his strength went rapidly and remorselessly on. The black days in which he could see no one were more frequent now; the visits of friends dwindled away and stopped completely. The heavy doses of sedatives ceased in the end to perform their function. He lay in his last extremity. Then, on the grey dawn of November 8, the room which had witnessed the final unhappy struggles of his burdened spirit fell silent; and the lad who had set out on the train to Woodstock that golden September morning long ago had at last finished his journey.

CANADIAN UNIVERSITY PAPERBOOKS

Of related interest

Lightning Source UK Ltd.
Milton Keynes UK
UKHW012358200722
406167UK00001B/323